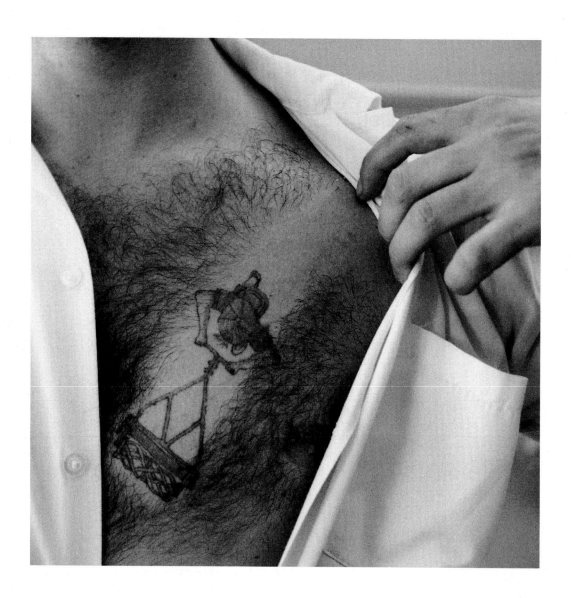

I Love Mom

AN IRREVERENT HISTORY OF THE TATTOO

J o h n   G r a y

CANADIAN CATALOGUING IN PUBLICATION DATA

Gray, John, 1946–
I love Mom: an irreverent history of the tattoo

ISBN 1-55013-581-3

1. Tattooing – History.   I. Title.

GN419.3.G73 1994   391'.65   C94-931451-X

Key Porter Books Limited
70 The Esplanade
Toronto, Ontario
Canada M5E 1R2

The publisher gratefully acknowledges the assistance of the Canada Council, the Ontario Arts Council and the Ontario Publishing Centre in the publication of this work.

Design: Scott Richardson
Typesetting: MacTrix DTP
Printed and bound in Canada

94 95 96 97 98 6 5 4 3 2 1

CONTENTS

Introduction: You're Thinking of Getting a *What?* / 9

SECTION ONE: IN THE BEGINNING / 21
The First Tattoo / 23
The Tattooed Boy: One / 27
The Fashionable Outlaw / 33
Thou Shalt Not / 53

SECTION TWO: MOVING BETWEEN THE LINES / 59
The Tattooed Boy: Two / 61
Colors for the Naked Ape / 69
The Tattooed Boy: Three / 79
Savages / 85

SECTION THREE: GETTING VISIBLE / 109
The Tattooed Boy: Four / 111
The Tattooed Man Redux / 115
The Tattooed Boy: Five / 127

Captions for Archival Illustrations / 140
Bibliography / 141
Photographer's Acknowledgments / 142

The Tattoo

Born a momentary flash,
Evidence of rude events;
Judgement rash, squandered cash,
Rash of youthful impudence;
To inscribe your indiscretion,
Veteran of stage and screen;
To record your proud progression,
Marching to the guillotine.
Mark now Nature's fatty rolls,
The coarser hair on lip and back;
Hateful holes, malicious moles,
Drooping wattles soft and slack —

From flaking scalp to horny toes,
I am the only mark you chose.

— JOHN GRAY, 1993

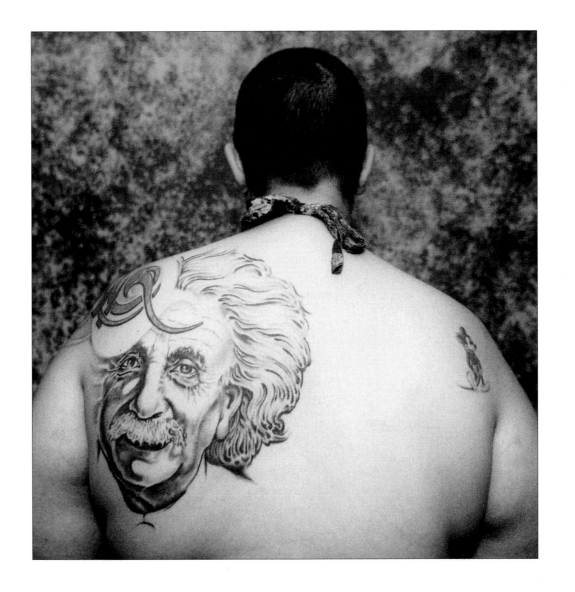

8

INTRODUCTION

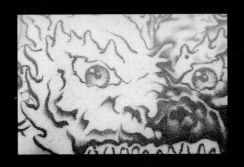

A BEE IN THE BONNET

An 1804 *irezumi* contest set a record for the largest tattoo —
a dragon that stretched across the torsos of twenty men side by side.
The Japanese judges, unimpressed by sheer size, gave the annual
award for Best Tattoo — envelope please — to a bee placed
delicately on the tip of a penis.

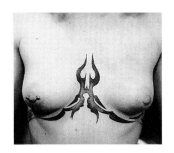

YOU'RE THINKING OF GETTING A *WHAT*? ♥

NOTHING EVOKES THAT SUPERIOR SHUDDER, THAT ANAL-RETENTIVE CLUCK OF CIVILIZED disapproval, quite like a tattoo.

Find out for yourself: in casual conversation with a relative or colleague mention casually, as though an afterthought, "By the way, I'm thinking of acquiring a tattoo."

After the pause you will hear something like "What are you thinking of doing *that* for?", murmured with the inflection of "Why would you want to pull out all your teeth?"

Now switch to a neutral topic — a recent movie or the price of real estate. Note the lingering chill in the basement of the conversation, a vaguely sectarian distance, as though you had just declared yourself a Scientologist.

To complete the experiment you will need a point of comparison, a control. Try this:

Under similar circumstances, turn to a family member or business associate and declare, "I'm thinking of having a surgeon slice the pouches from under my eyes," or "I want to have bags of silicone sewn into my breasts."

Quite another response: concern about your self-esteem, perhaps; or reassurance as to the state of your pouches or bustline; be yourself, beauty only skin deep, etc. Even when laced with contempt (vanity, vanity), the reaction will not vibrate with that hum of theological alarm that accompanied the subject of tattooing.

While having animal tissue injected into one's lips with a needle the size of a bug sprayer, or artificial hairs poked into one's skull may not receive enthusiastic applause, these urges are treated as symptoms of a mild psychological crisis, endearing evidence of a vulnerable, insecure nature.

A tattoo, however, is a threat.

Unlike cosmetic-surgery enthusiasts, tattooees seek not to conform to a conventional standard of beauty, but to distance themselves from the rest of us, to join an alien opposition.

People either have tattoos or they do not. A tattoo does not win friends among the untattooed majority. A tattoo is no way to get ahead.

A DIRTY BUSINESS

Tattooing has always emitted an unsavory aura in Western culture — a whiff of the criminal, the carnival sharp, the fallen woman, and the unhygienic lover.

"Tattooed Thracians are not well-born," sniffed Herodotus, the father of history, in the fifth century B.C. (According to Plutarch, Thracian women acquired tattoos as a souvenir of Orpheus, whom they tore to pieces in a fit of pique over his homosexual preferences.)

"Well-born" indeed! Today, tattoos are a common fetish of the shave-and-puncture subculture, to go with radiation-victim haircuts and multiple rings of surgical steel in nostrils and nipples — visual codes, no doubt, for unseemly sexual enthusiasms.

According to the media, tattooing is about to go permanently mainstream. Don't believe it. Rumors of imminent respectability have been chasing the tattoo for a century. When respectable people acquire tattoos, and they do, it's not because the practice has become respectable; it's because the recipient wishes inwardly to be *not* respectable, seeking out acts of private outrage that won't adversely affect the career path.

It doesn't matter what the tattoo is — a dedication ("I Love Mom"), a motto ("Death Before Dishonor"), a vow ("Property of Vito"), a warning ("Fuck Off"), a death symbol, predatory or mythical animal, flower, patriotic gesture, cartoon character, pinup girl, automotive logo, or primitive tribal scrawl. It's not the subject but the *fact* of a tattoo that contains its stigma and appeal. The tattooee has chosen to have an image indelibly stamped on his or her hide for no apparent reason other than a desire to be different.

What's wrong with the rest of us? Who do they think they are?

For a quasi-medical practice that entails injecting a foreign substance into a wound, the tattoo parlor is a breathtakingly unregulated industry. Although the city health inspector may call now and then to update the crumbling certificate on the wall, only the tattooist's personal ethic prompts him or her to maintain sanitary premises, wear surgical gloves, use new needles, and learn the medical effects of the various pigments. (It is not unknown for amateurs and semiprofessional "bootleggers" to use house paint!)

Given the Darwinian, *laissez-faire* nature of the craft, it's a testament to human probity that there exist any standards at all: that most tattooists turn away clients who are drunk, stoned, warped, or underage; refuse to mark "public skin" (above the neck or below the wrist); and usually refuse racist slogans, Nazi emblems, ill-advised vows, and obscenities. Such restraints are voluntary, however, and like most discretionary industrial standards of safety and cleanliness, apt to slip during an economic downturn.

In addition to medical qualms, there is every reason to fret about aesthetic standards, for nothing publicly or professionally identifies the impeccable craftsman or incompetent scratcher. Tattooists earn no degrees or fellowships; no magazine critics review their work. For the buyer there is no trial period, no guarantee, no five-year warranty on parts or labor.

Not that the average patron is fussy. Statistically, the majority of tattoos result from a momentary, possibly drunken, impulse (although the desire may have been present for some time), and tattoo parlors are chosen primarily on the basis of

NO BOOZE, NO DRUGS,

NO ONE UNDER 18 YEARS OF AGE,

WITHOUT PARENTAL OR LEGAL PERMISSION.

YES TATTOOS HURT.

NO THEY DON'T RUB OFF.

RATES:

80.00 per hour

40.00 minimum

30.00 deposit on

all appointments and / or

custom artwork / drawing.

geographical convenience. As a rule, more thought goes into the purchase of a stereo than a tattoo.

With predictable results. Face it — most tattoos look dreadful. A few years after application, these ill-considered icons of crude personal symbolism have blurred into dirty blobs of ink with hairs growing from them, as meaningful and attractive as a large strawberry mole.

OH, WHAT THE HELL

Despite these obvious drawbacks, approximately ten percent of the adult population choose to have themselves marked for life.

Why would they do that?

It's inadequate, though tempting, to dismiss them as mildly insane. Although psychiatrists usually view tattoos as symptoms of mental trouble, inmates of mental institutions have fewer tattoos than do the outside population. (On the other hand, it has been said that the three traits common to psychopathic serial killers is that they are male and white and they possess a tattoo.)

While it is no great challenge to understand why a person would not acquire a tattoo, the reasons why people *do* are interesting, contradictory, and elusive.

Like other persistent cultural practices just outside publicly acknowledged art, such as circuses, soap operas, and rock and roll, tattooing draws from deep wells in the collective and subjective consciousness. A cultural weed growing without encouragement, it is nourished by primitive needs. To frighten off an attacking enemy. To invoke magic or borrow power from another being. To ward off evil. To attract good fortune. To draw attention and sexual respect by means of an exaggerated plumage. To declare oneself different from, or part of, a tribe. To make permanent a decision or rite of passage. Tattooing is a complex act — social, sexual, mystical, and cosmetic.

The one fact about a tattoo that never varies is its permanence. There's no such thing as a temporary tattoo. Yes, tattoos can indeed be erased, but the resulting patch of scar tissue is as conspicuous as the mark it replaced.

People receive a tattoo *because* of its permanence. All tattoos represent a desire for a reality that endures despite our wrinkling skin and mutating identities. All tattoos, ugly or beautiful, Jesus Christ or Tweety Bird, represent the same urge: to transcend.

♥

Subconsciously, in an absurd, naive, slapstick fashion, people who receive tattoos are searching for God.

Think about it: a prominent 1930s' tattooist named Jack Redcloud displayed a large bust of Jesus, complete with bleeding crown of thorns, *upon his bald head.*

20

in the beginning

AHEAD OF THE COMPETITION

A feature of Maori tattooing was the practice of moki — covering the entire head
with detailed designs in many colors. Maori warriors placed great value on
these heads, and collected them as war trophies.

Although Western visitors shied away from having their own heads embellished in
this way, there developed a brisk trade in preserved, tattooed Maori heads as souvenirs
and lucky charms, until Europeans banned moki traffic in 1831.

By then, commercialization had coarsened the trade: one European trader,
upon expressing dissatisfaction with the quality of the tattooed head offered by a
Maori chief, was given his choice of the heads of the chief's still-living
assistants. Satisfaction guaranteed.

THE FIRST TATTOO

SOME PEOPLE CAN NEVER DO ANYTHING RIGHT. FROM THE DAY THEY'RE BORN THEY FEEL out of line, out of time, out of step. They get no encouragement. Notice from the Boss is never favorable.

Cain was a farmer. He made the Lord an offering of the "fruit of the ground." With scant selection in the burnt-offering department, what was he supposed to offer, *crêpes suzette?*

Besides, it's the thought that counts. Or so Cain thought.

Inexplicable as always, the Lord rejected Cain's offering of fresh garden produce in favor of the lamb offered by his younger brother, Abel. (The "fat portions" no less

— no vegetarian, He.) When Cain mildly protested this blatant example of primal paternal favoritism, the Lord sniffed that Cain was just going to have to try harder, wasn't he?

Then, as now, sycophancy was the key to success in a universe ruled by capricious, inscrutable whim. Then, as now, it could drive a person crazy.

This was all new to Cain, of course — Abel was always a bit more on the ball. Cain lost his bearings and performed a rash act, the deed that can never be undone, lashing out blindly at Abel's smug smile. And why not? There were no laws then. Nobody had said you shouldn't kill people, let alone that you were your brother's keeper.

Suddenly Abel was pushing up daisies, and Cain, like Adam and Eve before him, was in trouble with that totalitarian, desert chieftain of a deity — Jehovah, the mutton fancier, who invented inexplicable rules at whim, then punished you when you broke them.

At least that's how it must have seemed to Cain:

> **"My punishment is greater than I can bear. . . . I shall be a fugitive and a wanderer in the earth; and it will come to pass that whomsoever findeth me will slay me."**
>
> — GENESIS 4:13-14

It's not clear "whomsoever" was lurking out there to threaten the first-born progeny of Adam and Eve. Some precocious primate, maybe, an Abel type, eager to ingratiate himself with his Maker and improve his station.

Whatever the potential threat to Cain, the Supreme Being, Creator of the universe, took it seriously enough to bully Whomsoever with a threat of His own:

> **"Therefore whomsoever slayeth Cain, vengeance shall be taken on him sevenfold." And the Lord set a sign for Cain, lest any finding him should smite him.**
>
> — GENESIS 4:15

So God marked Cain with a divine hex, in the form of a tattoo — a celestial labor-saving device that freed up His energy and attention for more important things, such as what grade of lamb He preferred, and how well done.

Paradoxically, God's shameful mark transformed Cain. He was a special person now: his tattoo condemned him, protected him, and made him famous. No longer a petulant adolescent lout, he was a committed rebel.

Cain had an identity. Charisma. Cain's tattoo made him a star.

The first parent.

The first toady. The first rebel.

The first crime of passion.

The first outcast.

The first tattoo.

East of Eden.

James Dean.

♥

A CHECKERED CAREER

A South African wrestler named Jacobus Van Dyn, having difficulty establishing himself in America, had his head tattooed with a dragon covering his skull, and bows, arrows, and sprays of flowers on his face. He then entered the ring as "The Masked Marvel." However, The Masked Marvel failed to ignite the public imagination. Desperately short of funds and too committed in appearance for a career change, the unfortunate Van Dyn was reduced to offering his head to professional tattooists, to be delivered as a moki-like curio upon his demise in return for a fee right then.

Unexpected salvation from this fate came thanks to Al Capone. Impressed by the man's size and fearsome demeanor, Capone took the ex-wrestler on as his personal bodyguard. Thanks to his association with the notorious gangster, Van Dyn spent so many years in prison that he was able to successfully re-enter the wrestling arena, having changed his title from "The Masked Marvel" to "The Worst Man in the World."

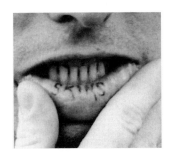

THE TATTOOED BOY: ONE ♥

YOU ATTENDED AN ELEMENTARY SCHOOL DEVOTED TO THE PURSUIT OF ORDER, DISCIPLINE, and success — a back-to-basics paradise. It was your first encounter with the world, unprotected by Mother.

Your lesson began in kindergarten, the day your class was instructed to make little sailboats by folding and pasting construction paper. Having seen pictures of sailboats, and therefore aware that they have keels, you left one corner of the paper hanging below your boat, contrary to instructions.

For this innovation you were made to sit in the corner. The eyes of your classmates pierced your back like pins.

In later weeks you occupied the corner for such offenses as failing to queue, insufficient neatness, and failing to pay attention. Small wonder; it was a challenge just to keep track of the myriad rules that buzzed erratically about the room like stinging insects.

But as the corner gave way to the strap, you learned to sense the direction of the prevailing wind, and by the time you entered Grade Two you blended perfectly amid the shiny pink faces, stupid as worms and passive as moss.

Like an underage Houdini you had learned to disappear. Thirty or forty years later, you can still vanish from a room, or even a group photograph. Look — your smile is indistinguishable from the others. You are there but unseen. Say cheese.

But not everyone disappeared quite so readily. For some, the threat of physical and psychological pain, the arbitrariness of it all, brought out something more primitive and more precious even than the will to survive.

The tattooed boy was on his third foster home by the time he joined your Grade Two class. The day he arrived, he carved his name in his desk with a stolen penknife.

This form of personal expression was not uncommon — all school desks were extensively etched with hearts-and-darts, crosses, stars, and *other people's* initials. But only the tattooed boy was so daring — or so stupid — as to put his own signature to the crime.

The tattooed boy slouched to the front of the classroom to face the teacher. The other children wagged their downy little heads contemptuously left to right in unison, the Elect, bound for Heaven. He had been caught. He was going to Hell. At the age of seven.

The tattooed boy received a strapping, one of several he endured that year as

you and your classmates looked on — identical, compliant stares hiding your sadistic excitement, the sensuous smugness of conformity.

For the first time you sensed the sexual undertow of grade-school discipline, the erotic component of physical power and pain. If you close your eyes, you can still see Teacher's flinty half-smile. She can't have been older than thirty-five, but in memory she appears as ageless and implacable as an Egyptian deity. The tattooed boy stands before her stomach, staring up. From his perspective, her breasts are so enormous they conceal her face.

I won't cry, can't make me.

A suspended moment of delicious tension, her hand almost gently holding his, then that sudden, stinging whack — again, again, again. Climax. The tattooed boy's crimson cheeks, muscles rigid, burning with pain and defiance. I won't cry, can't make me.

Later that year he covered his arms with crosses, swastikas, skulls-and-crossbones, using a ballpoint pen he had stolen from the corner drugstore.

His foster father stormed into class — a red-haired psychologist with rimless glasses and eczema over one eyebrow. (He had taken the boy on as a professional demonstration.) He confiscated the pen and bawled out his charge in front of everyone. The man was hysterical, desperate; even Teacher looked embarrassed.

You and your fellow angels watched this spectacle of raging parental failure, nodding righteously, reinforcing the seriousness of the crime. He was a Bad Boy.

The tattooed boy stared into the middle distance, cheeks bright red, jaw quivering, hands — covered with symbols whose meaning he had no way of understanding — clenched on the desk in front of him, just holding on.

♥

DEVIL ON HIS BACK

Several weeks after George Burchett tattooed a large red devil on his back, the client returned with a complaint: "I've had nothing but trouble since you put this thing on me. Something must be done."

Burchett explained that covering or removing such a large tattoo was out of the question. After consultation, he and his client reached a novel solution: tie the devil down with a tattooed chain. One end went around the devil's neck, the other was attached securely around the client's ankle.

The image adjusted, our man left in an optimistic mood.

Weeks later, he was back: "Sorry, but Satan is still doing a lot of abracadabra back there."

As a surefire device to make him behave, Burchett tattooed a cross on the *Devil's* back — a kind of mystical leapfrog.

The charm seems to have succeeded, for the client did not return.

THE FASHIONABLE OUTLAW   ♥

As did the Lord to Cain, so the Greeks, Romans, and Japanese routinely tattooed, branded, and otherwise permanently marked criminals, slaves, and other undesirables. The practice minimized paperwork, keeping track of troublemakers and social outcasts without expending too much official energy. (In the case of Caligula, the punishment had entertainment value as well: he is said to have forcibly tattooed people for fun.)

As a disciplinary measure, tattooing was relatively progressive. In thirteenth-century Japan it replaced the loss of an ear or a nose — useful when dealing with repeat offenders. By the Edo period (1603–1867), a first offense merited a horizontal line, a second an arch-shaped stroke, and a third another line. The three lines, taken together, formed the Japanese character *inu*, meaning "dog."

The relative mildness of the punishment encouraged conservative authority figures to tattoo other socially questionable groups — prostitutes, entertainers, and people who slaughtered animals.

If only as a means of reclaiming the self from arbitrary and unsympathetic definition, the obvious response to such permanently degrading symbols was to confuse, embellish and/or cover them with tattoos of the wearer's choosing. This impulse gave rise to an underground craft called *irezumi*, practiced semiprofessionally by underemployed printmakers.

Like so many bastard art forms from the wrong side of the tracks, *irezumi* redeemed a public liability, endowing its disreputable possessor with bravado and dash. An ornate assortment of dragons (strength), flowers (happiness), and spirals (eternity), pushed painfully and slowly under the skin with needles on the end of a stick, marked the social daredevil who made his conventional counterparts appear pallid and dull.

As the custom took hold and designs became more elaborate — the aesthetic image placed to move with the underlying musculature — the process functioned as a demonstration of physical courage, an implied challenge to the untattooed majority.

After all, what is at the root of conformity and respectability, if not personal cowardice and the fear of pain?

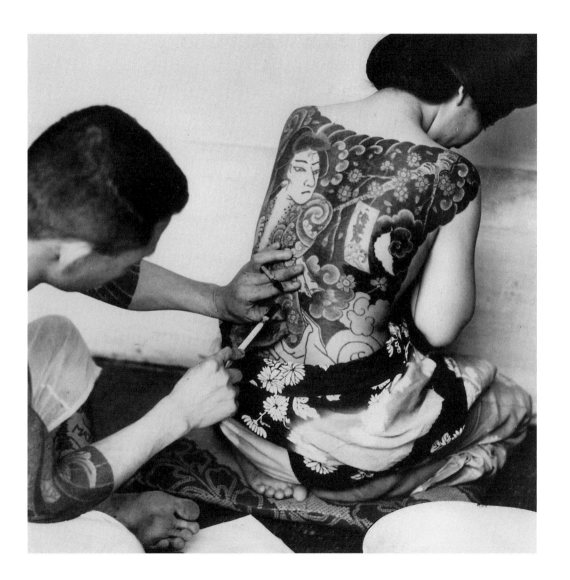

The movement of a cultural statement from one class to another is always triggered by a signal event. Such was the appearance of an eighteenth-century Chinese novel called *The Suikoden*, a Robin Hood story of 108 outlaw-heroes in revolt against wealth and corruption that became an enormous bestseller in Japan. The Japanese translation came lavishly illustrated with woodblock prints, in which the backs of the most popular and charismatic outlaws were adorned with dragons and tigers.

Fashionable members of the literate social classes, bored with mummified ritual art forms and attracted by the magnetic irony of the antihero, queued up for similar tattoos, conferred by "*irezumi* artists" who had honed their skills on criminal camouflage.

Suddenly, the tattoo had cachet. Like Paris fashion shows and Hollywood's Academy Awards, tattoo competitions celebrated the "best" *irezumi*. "Star" tattooists conferred such status upon clients that their tattooed skin, flayed and pickled, was bequeathed as a family heirloom — numbered and signed, of course.

Irezumi flourished until the mid-nineteenth century, when it was abruptly banned by Emperor Meiji, who worried that European trading partners, lacking Japanese sophistication, might view the practice as barbaric. Tourism, however, is a two-sided colonial weapon; it inhibits the culture of the host country while providing a tonic to the jaded traveler. British naval officers and other novelty-conscious visitors appreciated exotic decadence and radical dash as part of the tourist experience.

Not only sailors, but also upper-class passengers who paid to go on naval junkets to foreign lands, came home sporting these fashionable curiosities, authenticating their tales of adventure among the heathens.

Like contemporary tabloid descriptions of wild antics of the rich and famous, newspapers eagerly featured lurid accounts of aristocrats' tattoo experiences: elaborate, sharp-pointed instruments, rivers of blood, naked white bodies writhing in delicious agony under the inscrutable gaze of Orientals capable of anything. Toss in the risk of death by gangrene or syphilis, and readers simply couldn't get enough.

Magic Markers

As often occurs in pop culture, the foreign itch of the moment revealed a deeper domestic longing.

Despite the exhibitionist narcissism that characterized the tattoo rage in Europe, tattooing never strayed far from its primitive function as a source of supernatural power and a hex against danger. (The power of an icon is never far from hand — what twentieth-century person would deny the animate power of the swastika, hammer and sickle, or Coca-Cola logo?)

For the nineteenth-century British sailor, a tattooed pig or rooster protected against drowning (an ironic device, perhaps, for both creatures are notoriously poor swimmers); a swallow signified a message from home; a pair of open eyes on the pectorals ensured alertness during a long watch; and hinges tattooed near a joint added strength to the limb.

A cross on the back was a popular hedge against the cat-of-nine-tails — a tactical charm to soften the heart of the Christian torturer. (Practical, too: to keep sailors on their toes, a favored disciplinary measure was to flog the last man down from the masthead, no matter how quickly the sail was lowered.)

For a scion of the English upper classes, with a bleeder in the family and a drooler in the attic, tattooing drew on the imputed genetic strength of the lower, mongrel classes — like the then-fashionable practice of marrying one's coachman or chambermaid.

Of course, the upper classes were careful to usurp the proletarian spirit in a style that would distinguish them from true riff-raff, favoring imagery known to their accommodating tattooists as "high-class groteskew." By the 1890s, high-priced "tattoo parlors" had materialized in the better sections of London, where "tinting" was offered by "professors" such as George Burchett, "King of Tattooists."

Burchett, the son of an antique dealer, claimed to have started his life's work as a child in Brighton, tattooing gullible school friends with his mother's darning needles and a crude ink of soot suspended in sea water. Later, while a seaman on HMS *Victory*, he received tattoos from Hori Chiyo, the most famous Asian tattooist of the day. (Operating out of a bungalow in Yokohama, Hori Chiyo advertised his services in English tourist guidebooks. His shop door displayed the undertaking: "I Do Not Business If Fuddled.")

Back in England, having honed his skills on sausages, dead chickens, and the epidermis of his unfortunate wife, Edith (who is still considered a saint by tattooists), Burchett set up shop in Jermyn Street, tattooing the gentry for outrageous fees. He wore a white medical smock, and was surrounded by attractive if unspecifically trained female assistants modeling nurses' uniforms, creating a hygienic, luxurious atmosphere not unlike that of a society dentist or cosmetic surgeon.

After writing his memoirs, the "King of Tattooists" died in 1953 — on Good Friday, appropriately.

But for all their social and artistic posturing, Mayfair tattooists like Tom Riley, George Burchett, and Sutherland MacDonald (who coined the term "tattooist": "tattooer" had a working-class sound) were crude scratchers with only the most superficial grasp of the aesthetics of Japanese imagery. Most of their tattoos, unlike the designs they bastardized, were unrelated, badge-like emblems — some rather elegant, most corny and stereotypical — scattered over the pelt with no regard for continuity or the contours of the human body.

None of the Victorian tattooists learned Japanese shading techniques; as a result, their imagery remained inanimate, like gargoyles plastered on public buildings. The outlines, usually applied with a worn needle, tended to blur in scar tissue, while fill-in pigments faded quickly, no doubt to lurk carcinogenically as mercury, cadmium, or lead deposits in the client's system.

Nevertheless, a steady stream of profitable work flowed through their prolific establishments: bouquets, vows, homilies, monograms, and professional trade insignia; family crests on shoulders, coats-of-arms on elbows, and an array of self-consciously exotic Asian symbols, such as the snake swallowing its own tail that adorned the plump white forearm of Lady Randolph Churchill, Sir Winston's mom.

More ethnically appropriate, if not more tasteful, was the portrait of William Shakespeare that graced the heaving bosom of the actress Ellen Terry.

One-Stop Shopping

On the other side of the Atlantic, the upper-class tattoo craze confined itself to New York City, where wealthy industrialists and stockbrokers acquired stodgy, self-righteously allegorical nudes depicting Wealth, Industry, and Prosperity.

American society women took to the fashion with greater style and enthusiasm after the advent of the abbreviated bathing suit. Popular tattoo imagery of this period, such as the butterfly, was to appear on the thighs, shoulders, and upper arms of bathing beauties, nature lovers, and flower children for the rest of the century.

Writer and critic Dorothy Parker wore a heart tattoo — one might have expected something witty — and her husband wore an elephant rampant. At the opposite end of the spiritual spectrum, Salvation Army women had the letters "S" and "A" tattooed on their elbows.

American and British women quickly grasped the tattoo's practical potential as a source of permanent beauty marks, arched eyebrows, pink cheeks, red lips, and mascara. Some also acquired permanent stocking seams and embroidery — a female

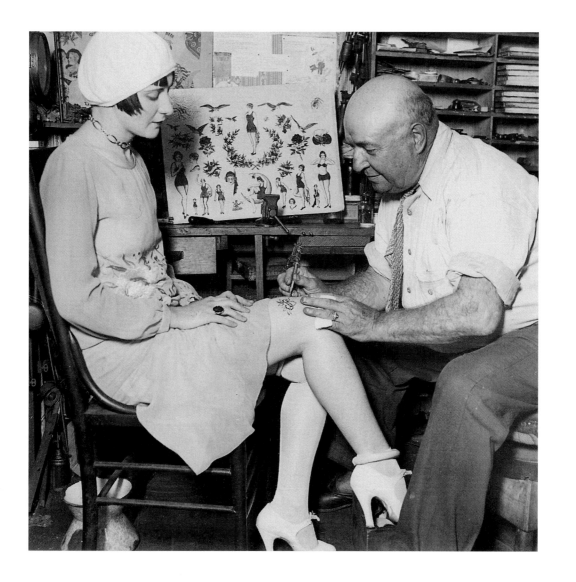

counterpart of the "Scotch socks" procured by thrifty gentlemen of the period. (Natives of Burma also wear Scotch socks — to ward off snakebite.)

By 1927, Los Angeles tattooist Henry Lawson and a group of cosmetic surgeons envisaged a coast-to-coast franchise dispensing hair design, body alteration, and tattooed cosmetics. A refined affair, the undertaking foundered in its infancy, victim of the 1929 crash.

We Weren't Always A Wimp

One would think the permanence of even cosmetic marking would have inhibited Victorians; yet, for even the most effete British aristo, coats-of-arms and other symbols contained Jungian race-memories of robust warrior ancestors. For the less well connected Victorian or American, even a timid tattoo became a romantic social ink blot test with which to distinguish friend from foe.

By the early part of the century, most of the royal males of Europe were tattooed: the future King George V of England and King George of Greece sported "Oriental" dragons by Ashton Taylor, another prominent tattooist to the Mayfair set; the Duke of Clarence (later a Jack the Ripper suspect) and the Duke of Saxe-Coburg-Gotha soon followed suit. Czar Nicholas of Russia was proudly punctured by Hori Chiyo, by then known as "the Shakespeare of Tattooing."

Prince George of England underwent eighty hours of tattooing to produce a dragon that covered his chest; it featured a precise representation of each feather on the wings.

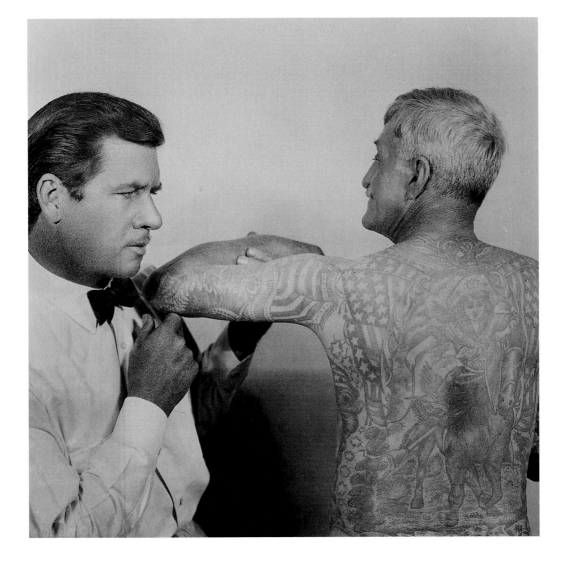

Despite his stylistic aping by the aristocracy, the outlaw, fashionable or not, remained an outlaw.

In Japan, *irezumi* fell into permanent disfavor as a perversely nonconformist gesture affected by firefighters and menial laborers, who were ashamed of having to bare their torsos in hot weather and wore tattoo "suits" to imitate clothing.

The practice was also adopted by the *yakuza*, the criminal underworld, no doubt to maintain spurious Robin Hood pretensions. (The stigma has endured. Even today, tattooed people are often denied entrance to Japanese public bathhouses as potentially disruptive.)

46

In Europe and North America too, even when tattoos were the height of fashion, their traditional stigmatic function endured, as nineteenth-century corrections administrators, military and civilian, inscribed the law of the land on the hides of offenders.

Inmates of the Massachusetts State Prison wore "Mass.S.P." and the date of their release on their left arms. After branding was abolished in 1717, British army deserters received the letter "D" and "men of bad character" — known homosexuals and dissipates — wore the initials "B.C." These tattoos were administered using a sprung-metal instrument pressed against the skin; with the release of a catch, needles shot forward to puncture the area.

While the practice of tattooing prisoners continued into this century in concentration camps and gulags, within the conventional penal system the tattoo became a fashion accessory, a tribal mark, and an existential survival tool.

Stripped, like Cain, of personal identity and marked by another, one's obvious response is ritual reversal and symbolic defiance: "You can't define me. I define myself." Like thirteenth-century Japanese felons, European and American offenders embellished their offending marks with other designs — first self-administered, then executed by semiprofessionals on the inside, later to be repaired by professionals.

The upper classes gave tattooing its high-end glamor; outlaws provided its industrial base.

M A R K I N G   T I M E

♥

The two most prevalently tattooed social groups, sailors and prisoners, have always had a good deal in common; indeed, when naval press gangs routinely kidnapped men into military service, the distinction was a fine one. It is still not uncommon for the career serviceman to see himself as a social outlaw; a propensity for harming people and property can impede smooth social interaction with civilians.

Among sailors and prisoners, sexually suggestive tattoos became popular as a hedge against homosexuality during a long term exclusively in the company of other men. A skillful tattooist could make a nude or hula girl who would dance on the wearer's musculature, to roars of appreciation from an audience that took its fun where it could find it. A strategically located tattoo simulating female anatomical essentials could mitigate the psychological damage to sailors and prisoners driven by desperation into homosexual activity.

Both the prisoner and the military man marked the progress of their lives in lengths measured by faceless superiors — sentences, wars, beginnings and endings. In shackles and in uniform, tattoos came to commemorate rites of passage. In the navy, an anchor signified an Atlantic passage; a full-rigged ship, a journey around Cape Horn; a dragon, a Pacific crossing.

In French prisons, dots at the base of the thumb came to represent years spent inside (three accumulated dots became code for "Death To Police"), and career thieves proclaimed themselves with a butterfly. Today, convicts in North America wear a cross on the hand with lines emanating from it or one small tear at the corner of the eye for each year of incarceration. In women's prisons, vow tattoos declare pacts with allies and "marriages" to other inmates.

Outlaw tattoos always contain an element of bravado and defiance, concealed or blatant. Apaches — Parisian thugs commemorated in a dance of ritualized sexual brutality — had dotted lines tattooed around their necks with the caption "Executioner Cut Here"; Nervi — hoodlums from Marseilles — wore guillotines drawn on their backs with "My Last Walk" inscribed underneath. Should you encounter a Frenchman with playing cards tattooed on the hand, walk briskly in the other direction, for each of the four suits signifies a nefarious act: "I clubbed him to the ground," "I stabbed his heart," "I stole his money," "I buried him in the ground."

48

Law enforcement officers took a dim view of such decorations, which, when discovered, became an excuse for police brutality. American gangsters of the 1920s, hedging their bets, favored a discreet handcuff with a broken link.

Prison tattooists exhibit remarkable ingenuity in improvising tools of the trade. The motor from a cassette player or electric razor provides power, the outer tube of a ballpoint pen is filled with ink, and a sharpened guitar string produces the unique line of the "Joint Style."

Inevitably, however, what is stylish in one culture is gauche in another: like a shipboard romance, prison sentiments, declarations, and associations tend to fade on the outside; but the tattoos remain. Fully forty percent of tattooists' daily bread is cover work, disguising the once-proud symbols of reformatories and penitentiaries, and the needle tracks of drug addicts.

But no matter how skillful the camouflage, the wearer himself knows what lies underneath — the telltale signal of the outlaw. Cain, the marked man, the one who can never fit in.

NICE WORK IF YOU CAN GET IT

Tom Riley, an Irishman who invented the first electric tattoo machine in 1891,
became resident tattooist at London's Royal Aquarium, serving an astonishing array of royal
clients — including Oscar II and Olga of Sweden, Haalen VIII of Norway, Alfonso XIII of Spain,
and Kaiser Wilhelm II — for fees of up to two hundred pounds. Riley's needle was in demand
in the palaces of Indian maharajas, and in 1899 Princess de Chimay of Cairo summoned
him to Egypt for three months of intensive work, including a set of permanently red lips.
While in Egypt, Riley tattooed Kemal Atatürk, the Khedan Abbas II.

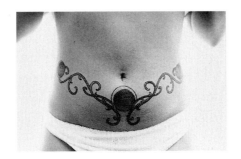

THOU SHALT NOT

♥

THE STORY OF CAIN MAY HAVE EVOLVED IN ORDER TO EXPLAIN THE TATTOOS OF A particularly ferocious, vengeful tribe called the Kenites. Jael, a Kenite woman, did away with a fugitive enemy Canaanite general by agreeing to hide him under a rug, then driving a tent peg through his head.

Nothing wishy-washy about Cain and Jael.

The expulsion of Cain is an earthly version of the fall of the Rebel Angels — victims of celestial office politics, in which the Creator finessed for power and control.

None of which makes sense in a monotheistic universe. The Jehovah of the Pentateuch (Genesis to Deuteronomy) existed in a firmament not unlike that of the early Greeks, competing with other gods for glory and adulation. Whether interpreted as myth, as metaphor, or as the big guy in the sky, however, this Lord is not a sympathetic character. Would you want Him as your immediate superior?

Likewise, the twelve tribes, having reached Canaan, found it an increasing struggle to sustain faith in their arid desert deity against the kinder, more supportive, and more relevant gods of an agricultural way of life.

Getting Tough

You could tell when an Israelite had lost faith in Jehovah: first he carved wooden objects and bowed down to them; then he acquired a tattoo.

Tattooing the hand was a feature of worshippers of the upwardly mobile Baal, Canaanite god of life and fertility, who ultimately seized power from Yamm, the sea god; created a palace with the help of Kothar, god of arts and crafts; and went on to become the Greek god Belos, better known as Zeus.

The Hittite, Canaanite, Egyptian, and Babylonian gods were a colorful, artsy, festive crowd — a merry contrast to the reclusive, dour, jealous Jehovah, who bore an unflattering resemblance to the Sumerian deity Mot, god of famine, sterility, and death.

For a growing number of disenchanted Israelites, the tattoo functioned a bit like intermarriage, as a permanent break with an outmoded past. Put enough tattooed men and women together and you have a tribe within the tribe — people who, like Cain, are not on the Lord's team.

Predictably, Jehovah responded to such public disenchantment with yet another law:

> **Ye shall not make any gashes in your flesh for the dead or tattoo any marks upon you: I am the Lord.**
>
> — LEVITICUS 19:28

But even with divine rules governing the accretions and excretions of every waking moment, with threats of pestilence, famine, and enslavement, and the continual tongue-lashings of apoplectic prophets, the Israelites regularly backslid into paganism. Barely two decades after the reign of Solomon, only two of the twelve tribes kept the faith (and even they were growing tentative), while the rest of Israel carved images to Baal, Astarte, Asherah, and a variety of Sumerian and Babylonian deities.

It is said that Jehoiakim, pagan ruler of Israel after its separation from the intermittently reverent kingdom of Judah, thumbed his nose at Jehovah by ordering the divine name tattooed on his penis, with which he then committed incest. That such a story was conceivable, even as apocrypha, suggests that the God of our imperfect understanding was never in power by popular demand. Given the chance, people deserted in droves.

Centuries later, it is claimed, He sent His gentler, more personable offspring to soften the message and buff up the holy image. Despite the success of the Christian Messiah, His coming was a fiasco for Dad, resulting in more dissention, acrimony, bloodshed — and tattooing — than ever.

Maybe next time.

A second-century A.D. Gnostic sect called the Cainites, in the eastern Roman Empire, interpreted the Old and New Testaments to reveal that the Lord was not merely a fraud but positively wicked, having created the world as a diversionary tactic to prevent mankind from ever knowing the true, indescribable Creator, the Real Thing. In other words, according to the Cainites, Judeo-Christians were worshipping the Devil by mistake.

With early Christians served up as lions' lunch, it must have been tempting to see Jesus as a cruel hoax, a spiritual booby-trap. Accordingly, for the Cainites, salvation could be reached only by *breaking* the laws of the Lord. In their view, the true hero of the Bible was not the Son of God but — you guessed it — our man Cain, the eternal wanderer.

This perverse reading of scripture made so much more sense to so many people that the Christian Creed was hammered out in large part to put an end to Gnostic theological speculation.

The Lamb of God had descended to earth, but the tattooed man just wouldn't go away.

Cain never liked lamb.

moving between the lines

BETTER READ THAN RED

A patriotic Chicago doctor named Andrew Ivy, at the height of the Cold War, thought it
would be prudent to tattoo every man, woman, and child in America with name, blood type,
and Social Security Number, in order to facilitate identification in the event of an atomic attack.
American media, in a frenzy thanks to McCarthy and Khrushchev, warmed to the idea,
and for a time it seemed feasible.

Dr. Ivy immediately set his mind to the problem of placement: since arms, legs, and heads
are apt to go missing in an atomic blast, it seemed appropriate to locate these identifying
tattoos on the torso; finally the doctor settled on the left ribcage as the most convenient
and least "visually annoying" surface, and the call went out for volunteers.

Unfortunately, Ivy had failed to consult professional tattooists, any one of whom could
have told him that the ribcage is easily the most painful part of the body to tattoo.
After early recipients passed out cold from the pain of the operation, the project languished
for lack of interest, and had to be called off.

THE TATTOOED BOY: TWO ♥

To BE ALIVE IN WESTERN CULTURE IS TO BE, SOONER OR LATER, VISIBLE; AND TO BE VISIBLE is to be judged. Even an absence — physical, mental, or spiritual — is noted, as it takes on a discernible shape, like a track in the snow.

In Grade Three you took a test. At first you thought it was a game, a puzzle, rather fun. Teacher did not share your delight. She took one look at your results and sent you to the principal.

Lights. Curtain. Showtime.

After a host of other tests, it was announced that you were a child with a Problem: you couldn't read, write, or add. In fact, you didn't seem to have learned a thing since that day in kindergarten when you made your paper boat with a keel.

The school's powerful remedial engine rumbled into motion. Gears shifted, cogs turned. Eyes were checked, ears tested. Your intelligence, perception, and emotional maturity were carefully gauged with calipers, charts, and a slide rule.

Results were interpreted. Nothing seemed measurably out of whack. You were not blind, deaf, or dumb, and as a member of a "good family" you couldn't be genetically "bad." Therefore you must be . . . lazy.

Lazy. Not a failure of the system, but an existential aberration. The lazy boy or girl was a uniquely contemptible creature: a middle-class, liberal offender; a soft, sneaky malefactor, as bad as a juvenile delinquent — even worse, for a juvenile delinquent could at least cite class warfare as a motive.

The work ethic, the heart and soul of North America, reserves a special cauldron in hell for laziness. Even vicious persons are reviled less than lazy ones, for the worst the vicious can do is murder someone. Laziness, on the other hand, knows no limit, demands no effort, and requires no equipment. Laziness is contagious, dragging others down in its muscular failure to resist evil.

You had become visible, identified, pegged like an insect on a pin. Word spread quickly. You recognized the contemptuous stares of your classmates. You had stared like that yourself, once.

At the tattooed boy.

Overnight, you were no longer among the Elect. You were going to Hell.

Sensing your peril, you resolved to claw your way back to respectability and invisibility in the collective womb. But as you slinked obsequiously down the

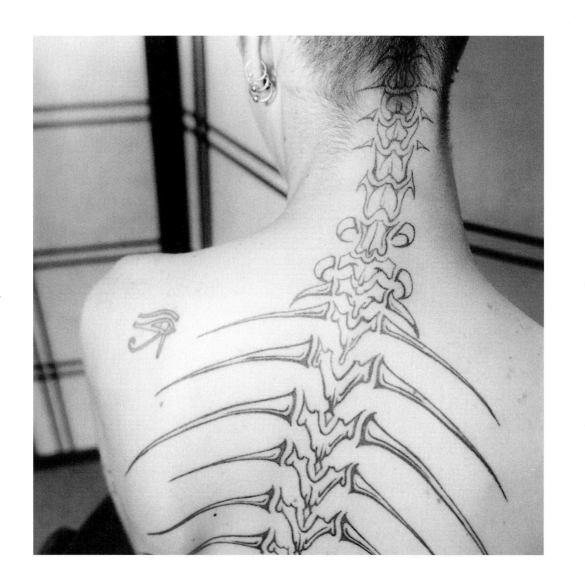

Dustbaned aisle to your desk each morning, your mind was already losing its way in the foggy corridors of boredom, and each class degenerated into a barrage of small humiliations.

Suddenly it was just you and the tattooed boy, crouched at the foot of the class. Lacking an identity of your own, you imitated his.

As schooldays passed like dripping tapwater, the two of you whiled away the time drawing wristwatches, military crosses, pentacles, skulls-and-crossbones, and swastikas on your arms with ballpoint pens — reflections of your motor skills, not your religion or politics. Occasionally you were sent to wash them off. In the washroom, you smoked.

By Grade Five you scored an E for neatness, and an F for "willingness and purpose to try hard all the time." In Grade Six you flunked music, even though your parents had spent a small fortune on your piano lessons. By Grade Seven, expensive private tutors had discovered that they might as well try to train a cat. Career counselors gently urged your frantic parents to direct their thinking to the Armed Forces, as a means to discipline and a trade — say, welding. (This prospect was not without appeal. You would join the navy and acquire a tattoo on the back of your hand, like the Tareyton cigarette man.)

You were outpaced by the tattooed boy: that spring the principal expelled him for smoking, and the police arrested him for shoplifting. "Please Excuse" forgeries were uncovered — and checks, as well.

The tattooed boy disappeared for several months. When he reappeared his pompadour was the most extravagant ever seen in the school: two precise parts, one above each ear, hair swelling in symmetrical waves, meeting and curling elegantly

♥

between the eyebrows, leaving a slippery residue on the forehead. (The effect took more than Brylcreem: only petroleum jelly had sufficient hold.)

He wore his shirt with the collar up and the two top buttons undone, displaying his hairless chest.

And his tattoos.

They went beyond bubblegum transfers and ballpoint pens. These things were real: simple, crude marks in India ink, self-administered, using three sewing needles stuck in an eraser. Iron Crosses and Xs and Os bedecked his chest, with "hot" and "cold" above the nipples. On his knuckles it said "love" and "hate," and between the thumb and forefinger he'd drawn a small Celtic cross, with a loop on top and lines emanating like cartoon surprise. Taste was not at issue here; these were declarations of independence.

When he offered you a tattoo in the design of your choice, using the sharpened point of a geometry compass, you knew he was calling for a commitment.

You were willing to imitate the tattooed boy, but not follow him. You lacked the courage to walk through the door and slam it shut. You were unwilling to proclaim yourself either Abel or Cain.

"I can't. My parents would kill me."

"Suit yourself," he shrugged.

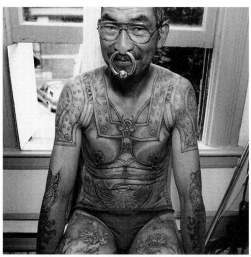
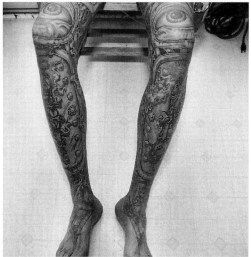

♥

THE INFLEXIBLE WOMAN

A New York stenographer named Mae Vandermark, on the advice of a Miss Pictoria,
was covered neck to ankle by a Coney Island boardwalk tattooer named Gus Wagner.
In 1924 she joined Ringling Brothers as "Miss Arturio," and became a celebrity.
For the 1927 summer tour, Ringling Brothers, in a bullish mood, took on another star
attraction, "The India Rubber Man." Clarence H. Alexander, formerly of Ypsilanti, Michigan,
could stretch his neck seven inches, and his arms and legs twelve inches each.
Ringling Brothers featured Miss Arturio and The India Rubber Man together, as part of an
all-star sideshow freak revue. The act enjoyed tremendous success, until The India Rubber Man
fell in love with Miss Arturio. He was forty-three, she twenty-two. Ungenerous circus wags
referred to them as "Tattooed May and Rubber November."
The India Rubber Man recognized in her a soulmate, a fellow exile from the salons of normality.
Miss Arturio disagreed: having chosen her appearance, she considered herself not a freak,
but an artist. The India Rubber Man, however, was born with his peculiarity. He was the freak.
Miss Arturio was repelled by his attentions, and complained bitterly to management.
Ringling Brothers turned a blind eye when he playfully used his elastic capability to pass
love notes to her, over the heads of the fat lady and the midget. But when he began declaring
his love publicly in word and in song, and bursting into tears during the show,
that was not entertainment.
The India Rubber Man was moved to another tent, on the theory that, deprived of a view
of her tattoos, the pliant performer would regain his composure.
Not so. He pined.
He took strychnine during a performance, and died on stage.

COLORS FOR THE NAKED APE ♥

THERE IS A THEORY AMONG ANTHROPOLOGISTS THAT TATTOOING COINCIDES WITH THAT elusive Darwinian cusp, the theoretical transition in personal grooming from ape to naked ape. According to this scenario, an embarrassed, hairless creature, up on his hind legs and exposed to the elements, seeks to protect and camouflage his pelt, and to identify himself as a member of his pack, with colors that will not fail him when it rains.

Which came first, the tribe or the rebel? Or did they arise simultaneously, the human paradox commemorated on the skin?

Those stylized horses that galloped over the arms and shoulders of our Scythian ancestors — dug out of peat bogs and glaciers like human truffles — were symbols of inclusion, not revolt. Prehistoric women of the South Pacific were tattooed on the lips and arms as a publicly sanctioned symbol of birth, copulation, and death. Four-thousand-year-old Egyptian mummies display tattooed dots and dashes on their thighs, abdomens, and arms like the stitches on dungarees, symbols of their attachment to the tribe and the world order.

In New Guinea, the ancient Roco society described untattooed people as "raw" — liable to rot, to revert to compost. The tattooed person was "cooked" — transformed by civilization into a social being, unlikely to return to a primitive state.

Today, new members are initiated into the Hell's Angels and other gangs with tattoos of their group's insignia, colors, and initials, as proof of their commitment to the gang and rejection of the rest of the world. Later, further biker tattoos permanently commemorate notable acts of daring that admit one to the elite within that gang, like the hands of New Guinea warriors marked to indicate the taking of a head.

Whether a mark of exclusion or inclusion, a tattoo has always signified power. Ainu women of Japan tattooed their faces not only to mark their passage into womanhood but also in imitation of male beards, to express their understandable desire to acquire some male power in a sexually stratified society. Chinese divers wore tattoos both as tribal symbols and to intimidate dangerous fish. Paris tattooed himself in the temple of Hercules so that the arrows of Menelaus, Helen of Troy's jealous husband, would not harm him.

Tattoos were administered by priests and shamans as a gesture of faith, a cosmic tetanus shot in a world without insurance. Arabs and the Haida wore tattoos

♥

as medicinal charms; the Cree tattooed crosses on their cheeks as a cure for toothache. Many still believe that tattooing functions as a remedy for rheumatism.

Where is that light?
Round about the King's house.
And the small laughter?
The small, merry laughter, it is
Of the sons and daughters of the
tattooed.

— HERMAN MELVILLE, *OMOO*

I DREAMT A DREAM

Often a tattoo was a message transferring power, not just from one time to another, but from one reality to another. The traditional American native cosmos more closely resembles an onion than a pyramid, each layer a world bustling with spirits, guardians, and demons. Passage from one world to another could be achieved in dreams, whose images were brought to this world in the form of tattoos.

Cree tattooists kept their instruments in a sacred bundle which they bequeathed to the heirs of their multiple calling: medical tattooing was a profession, decorative tattooing a trade, sacred tattooing a duty. The price of a decorative tattoo was one horse; but if the client was responding to a dream, the tattoo was administered free.

European sailors shared the aboriginal preoccupation with dreams and dream

imagery, which gave a lasting surrealist spin to the design process that remains to this day: what could be more surrealistic than an image joining together a dagger, a snake, a flower, and a naked woman, on the forearm of a man?

The Dyak tribes of Borneo believe that Apo-Kesio, their idea of Heaven, is a surreal world in which everything becomes its opposite — sweet becomes sour, hot becomes cold, light becomes dark. Dyak women tattoo themselves with the darkest pigments available so that, when the world reverses itself after death, their tattoos will shed light through the darkness and guide them to paradise.

Tattoos can have power even for people who know nothing about the dream world they represent. Roman legionnaires, goose-stepping their way through Gaul, were startled and fascinated by whole populations of tattooed people who looked as though they came from another planet. The word "Pict" derives from the name of the iron instrument with which these redheaded rascals performed their tattoos; the word "Briton" derives from the Breton word "brizzard," meaning "painted many colors."

Like British sailors and Asian nobles centuries later, Caesar's finest received tattoos as exotic memorabilia — impressive if incomprehensible — and as a way of borrowing that undiluted vigor we still attribute to "primitives," whether headhunters or longshoremen.

But as the Bible took hold in Northern Europe, the whims of Jehovah found their way into the criminal-justice system just as they had in the time of Moses. Each of the Lord's many little rules had its corresponding body-altering torture, from the removal of poachers' hands to the iron tweezers clamped onto the tongues of gossips. You could scarcely walk down the street without seeing some nonconformist whipped with a knotted rope or chained in an iron collar.

One of these little rules dated back to Constantine I, who banned tattooing around 320. Pope Hadrian I seconded the injunction at the First Council of Churches in Northumberland in 787. Early Christians viewed tattooing, accurately, as a symbol of paganism, of theological threat — thus was born the fear of heresy, one of the most dangerous public psychoses known, a little gift from Leviticus to mankind. The stigma gradually took hold, and during the Middle Ages tattooing virtually died out in Europe.

Even the Visigoths could take the hint.

It was as though the newly converted Christians of Northern Europe, like the Israelites in Canaan, knew deep down that their God was not an intrinsically salable commodity, that He was not going to bring them a whole lot of happiness — in short, that he didn't stand up to pagan competition.

Ergo, eliminate the competition altogether.

By 1066, only "vow tattoos" survived — period versions of "I love Mom" for the burn-rape-and-pillage set, the Hell's Angels of Gaul. (The rose-and-thorn virginity symbol, with banner and woman's name, remains a favorite today.)

Following the Battle of Hastings, the mangled corpse of King Harold was identifiable only by the inscription "I Love Edith" tattooed over his heart. The positive identification was made on the battlefield by "Edith of the Swan Neck" herself. She was very upset.

Ironically, it was primarily *religious* tattooing that kept the craft alive: crosses and other symbols were carved into the skin of Nestorian monks, and Crusaders eager to obtain a Christian burial should they die on Muslim soil. In homage to the Crusaders, later pilgrims to the Holy Land acquired religious tattoos, together with the word "Jerusalem" and the date of their visit — early versions of the "Rock of Ages" and

"Last Supper" tattoos that would become clichés in the twentieth century. Christian pilgrims' tattoos were executed by the same enterprising Gypsies who marked Muslim pilgrims to Mecca and Medina. The continuity of religious tattooing, in defiance of Mosaic, Christian, and Islamic law, suggests that the power of the image is enough to offset the sin of the act.

Throughout the Renaissance the decline continued, as tattooing became identified with a primitive imagination whose forms of expression had become *passé* in that heady period of scientific and cultural innovation. To the Renaissance man, the tattooed man was not only a pagan, but an unfashionable lout — as out of place at Hampton Court as a Hell's Angel at Bergdorf Goodman.

By the late seventeenth century, it seemed that tattooing was gone forever — that is, until "raw" Europeans discovered that they comprised a fragile minority in a tattooed world.

While priests were burning heretics in Belgium, natives in North and South America were busily rubbing color into scratches and knife slashes; their counterparts in Siberia and the subarctic used a needle and thread coated with soot and drawn underneath the skin. Around the Pacific Rim folks tapped pigment into their skin with miniature rakes, wooden-handled needles, and brass pen-like instruments with a slit point and a weight on one end.

During the Age of Discovery, adventurers from Marco Polo onward, like the Roman legions in Gaul, returned home tattooed with the symbols of more colorful, complicated, tolerant points of view. It was only a matter of time before Europeans recalled their long-suppressed pagan rituals of simultaneous inclusion and exclusion — in the barracks, jails, and low-life hangouts — hothouses for the culture of disgrace.

THE REARGUARD

Archduke Francis Ferdinand of Austria-Hungary was worried about his brother's tattoo. Crown Prince Rudolf had ordered a serpent over his heart to protect against gunshot wounds. Unfortunately, the tattooist positioned the serpent with its tongue facing away from the heart, the wrong direction to shield that vital organ. The archduke had received a similar serpent from the same tattooist, and it too was slightly out of position, but Francis Ferdinand's tattoo was located on the buttock — a far less critical area.

On June 28, 1914, Archduke Francis Ferdinand was assassinated by a Serb nationalist, Gavrilo Princip, at Sarajevo. The event touched off a war between Austria and Serbia, which blossomed malignantly into World War I, out of which arose Hitler and Stalin. A bad break for Francis Ferdinand, a bad break for the world.

The postmortem on the archduke revealed that the fatal bullet had passed straight through the middle of his serpent tattoo.

THE TATTOOED BOY: THREE   ♥

YOU AND THE TATTOOED BOY DESCENDED THE ACADEMIC LADDER IN TANDEM, REACHING the basement in Nine F, which was reserved for repeaters and juvenile delinquents — the gas station attendants, warehouse clerks, public assistance recipients, and felons of tomorrow. Sinewy and pale from hard work, often toothless from hard knocks, they sprang like weeds from the wrong side of the tracks — the land of broken marriages, occupational injuries, the working poor, the functionally illiterate, the stoned and drunk.

The tattooed boy fitted right in. Not you. You were merely lazy. Passive and bovine, you offended middle and lower classes in equal measure. You failed both

English and Industrial Arts; failed to write a complete sentence and to construct a match-scratcher. In gym, you were an enemy to your team.

In all fairness, you were never rude, never acted up; you just sat there — day after day, week after week, with a bland, noncommittal expression pasted on your mug, fleshy and passive, sweating freely with suppressed sexual desire. You were desperate to blend in or to disappear. You did neither.

The tattooed boy kept a condom in his wallet, in the section designed for business cards. It was always the same condom: he claimed to wash, powder, and reroll it after use, in the interests of thrift.

You tried. You bought a black leather jacket, unbuttoned the top three buttons of your shirt, turned up your collar, and wore your undershirt backwards. You pegged your trouser cuffs so tightly it took all your strength to pull them over your feet. You squeezed so much of Father's Wildroot onto your hair, your head foamed in the rain. You bought a condom, unrolled only in rehearsal.

No use. You had mastered the content of failure but not the style, the impenetrable belligerence with which the tattooed boy maintained his cool. Girls easily saw through your bourgeois politeness, your willingness to grovel — so unattractively unctuous and overeager to please. Teachers found you repulsive — to look at, to talk to, and to smell. You gave human form to the suspicion that their life's work was, in large measure, a failure.

The tattooed boy hulked just behind you at the back of the class, knees jutting into the aisle, front teeth missing, sullen, imposing, whispering filthy stories in your ear.

By now he wore more complicated tattoos, still self-administered with pins and India ink: vow (heart, rose and banner with girls' names), warning (snake, dagger,

♥

skull), and an anatomically preposterous female nude on the inside of his forearm. He was left-handed: consequently his most ambitious work appeared on his right arm.

Other classmates affected tattoos — and lived to regret it. Bobby Wilber returned from Detroit with a panther and "Walk on the Wild Side" on his shoulder. He later became an optometrist.

Your skin remained marked only by acne; like your mind and your future, it was a vacant lot.

Students kept a tactful distance from the tattooed boy. Teachers spoke to him rarely, discreetly, carefully. It was said that his tattoos had endowed him with supernatural strength: in a fistfight outside the Legion Hall dance, he broke an opponent's sternum with a flick of a tattooed wrist.

As high school dragged to its gowned conclusion he became more and more elusive, until one day, without warning, he was gone — just an empty desk with initials and drawings inscribed with penknife and geometry compass. The entire school system sighed with relief.

You had lost your only friend.

PRINTING: BY HAND MA

♥

There once was a harlot of Yale

Whose price was tattooed on her tail

While on her behind

For the sake of the blind

Was "REDUCTION FOR PARTIES" . . . in braille.

— ANONYMOUS

SAVAGES

♥

FRIDAY, AUGUST 3, 1492. THREE SHIPS, LOADED TO THE GUNWALES WITH CULTURAL AND spiritual baggage, disappeared over the edge of the known universe, carrying letters from the King and Queen of Spain to the Grand Khan of Cathay. Interpreters on board spoke Hebrew, Chaldean, and Arabic.

Instead of Asia, what they eventually found over the horizon was a "New World," populated by hitherto unknown life forms — moose, mosquitoes, skunks, rattlesnakes, and tattooed pagans with a world view that must have made Columbus shudder with dread. Thanks to the ongoing Spanish Inquisition, 8,800 burned at the stake for deviating from the family values of the day between 1478 and 1498. Back home in Barcelona, curiosity killed the cat.

> **And this tattooing had been the work of a departed prophet and seer of his island, who by those hieroglyphic marks had written out on his body a complete theory of the heavens and the earth, and a mystical treatise on the art of attaining truth. . . .**
>
> — HERMAN MELVILLE

In a sense, Columbus had it easy, compared to North American explorers. At least he found gold. Where others had hoped to find gold, silks, spices and plunder, they found instead a number of threatening, unanswerable questions:

Was the world not flat? Was Christian Europe not the center of the universe? Was God not on our side?

What did it all mean?

On what basis were they to spread the word of the Lord? How did one explain the paternalistic charms of the Aryan desert deity and his Son to a native population with no word for salt, prison, candle, or shepherd?

In 1578, Queen Elizabeth I of England was in the twentieth year of her reign. The Renaissance mind had begun to shed the dogmatic blinkers of the Middle Ages, and the world looked very different with peripheral vision restored.

That year, Martin Frobisher, back from another crack at the Northwest Passage, brought into London society a native woman with blue-black tattoos on her cheeks, chin, and forehead.

**About their legs strange lists they there doe
make, pricking the same with Needles, then
They take indelible tincture: which rubb'd in, the
Gallants doe account their bravest gin.**

— AN EXPLORER

This arctic woman — and the succession of tattooed foreign curiosities who followed her to Europe — although a typical, upright member of her own society, represented to Europeans the radical self-expression, physical vanity, and exuberant sexuality they had denied themselves (or pretended to), in the service of their restrictive deity. The tattooed pagan became the wet dream of an overheated imagination.

**The squaws use that sinful art of painting their faces
in the hollow of their eyes and nose, and their cheekbones on
which they have a blue cross dyed very deep.**

— AN EXPLORER

Throughout the following century, as the voyages of the *Discovery* and the *Endeavour* brought contact between Europeans and Polynesians, tattoos from Tahiti (from "tau-tau" — to mark) became highly sexual souvenirs of the exotic, proudly displayed by sailors upon their return. (Odd, isn't it, that the first two words to move from Polynesian to English usage were "tattoo" and "taboo"?)

The practice became such a staple of South Seas travel that Captain Bligh, following the *Bounty* mutiny, provided to Lord Cornwallis details of the tattoos

90

adorning Fletcher Christian and his fellow mutineers — including stars over the heart, hearts-and-darts on the arms, and a number of unspecific or unmentionable tattoos on the backsides — as an aid to identification and capture.

In 1769 James Cook brought to London a tattooed Polynesian named Omai, who became the most famous of the "tattooed savages" exhibited by pseudo-learned societies, presented by show-business entrepreneurs, and eagerly gawked at by paying audiences. (Commercial exploitation, certainly, but it was not always clear who was exploiting whom. Some warriors had traveled to England on the pretence of becoming Christian; what they were really after were muskets, which they intended to put to devastating advantage upon their return home.)

Ambitious European showmen soon got in on the act: John Rutherford claimed to have been captured by the Maori in New Zealand, where he married, settled down, and received a full complement of ritual tattoos.

True or not, it made a good story. Back home in London, he made a fortune.

Delicious tales of adventure became part of the ever-popular and profitable "tattooed man" exhibit, which by 1850 had become a vital part of that dark church of hocus-pocus, that quasi-mystical entertainment called the sideshow or carnival.

THE ILLUSTRATED MAN

The first "tattooed man" featured by P. T. Barnum was an Albanian-born Greek named George Constantine. Tattooed with 388 Burmese designs, he boasted the most complete and elaborate tattooing ever witnessed in Europe or America. He was covered literally from head to toe — eyelids, scalp, and the interior of his ears included. From a distance, he looked like a man dressed in an elaborately embroidered condom.

Constantine claimed to be descended from the first Christian emperor (ironic, for Constantine I had first banned tattooing in Europe). His dubious story was that he had been taken prisoner by "Chinese Tartars" in Burma while doing some illegal gold mining. He and three other prisoners were decorated as a brutal punishment administered by six tattooers over a period of six months. One of his colleagues died; another went blind.

Barnum brought Constantine to America in 1873, for an unheard-of stipend of a thousand dollars a week, and named him Captain Constantinus (in the circus tradition of military stage-names). Occasionally he was billed as "Prince Constantinus the Turk, the Living Picture Gallery." (The term "living picture gallery" subsequently became entrenched in circus tattoo exhibits all over the world.)

To an accompanying lecture delivered by a dermatologist named "Professor Hebra," Constantine swept onstage in majestic silence, wearing long braids, a loincloth, and a diamond solitaire ring. Professor Hebra inevitably concluded his spiel with: "And this wild tattooed man is always much admired by the ladies!" — a hint of eroticism that invariably brought down the house.

There is, however, no place like home. In 1887, Constantine abruptly reappeared in Constantinople on a U.S. passport, pretending to understand neither Greek nor Turkish and seeking an audience with the sultan as an "African wonder."

He was immediately recognized as a local rascal who had flown the coop back in 1860. The mortified Living Picture Gallery was taken to his sister's house, where

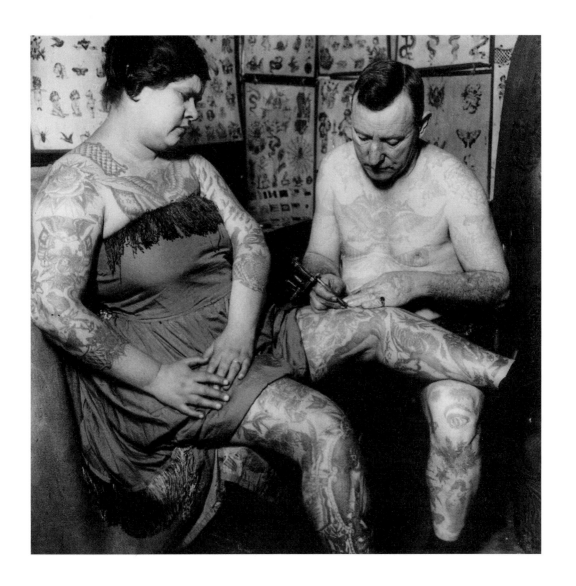

his family attempted to remove his tattoos with pumice stone, soap, and a laundry brush. A few days later, he disappeared without a trace.

Nice Work If You Can Get It

Despite his exposure as an elaborate fraud, the success of the Constantine act prompted other circuses to seek out tattoo exhibits. Careers were born as men with some tattooing on their bodies sought out tattooists to complete their "coverage." Becoming a picture gallery was an attractive career choice: in the big circuses, salaries of two and three hundred dollars a week were not infrequent. By comparison, a railroad laborer was paid $2.25 per day.

Tattoo exhibits became more elaborate, with mind-reading and juggling as added attractions. After the show, the tattooed man would set up shop, tattooing patrons and thereby increasing his income.

Along with the tattooed man came the inevitable tattooed lady. With a pseudonym like "Miss Pictura," she proved an even stronger attraction. (The most famous of these was a 1920s exhibit, "Lady Viola," with six presidents on her chest, the Washington Capitol on her back, and ten celebrities on her arms and legs — including Babe Ruth, Charlie Chaplin, and Tom Mix.)

There is no doubt many of these attractions involved weekly applications of stencil and paint. The jilted lover of Miss Jemima the Tattooed Girl is said to have avenged himself so that the unfortunate woman faced her public covered with such statements as "This Side Up" and "Handle With Care."

Following the depression of the 1880s, competition became vicious. Tattooed wrestlers and knife-throwers took the stage. Dwarfs and mutants — as though they hadn't suffered enough — were forced to acquire tattoos just to compete. One Coney Island sideshow featured a tattooed cow. Bet you wish you'd seen *that*.

You Know What They Say About Savages

Given the pagan origin of tattoo exhibits and the Christian origin of the spectators, a popular feature of the Tattooed Lady exhibit was an erotic, pseudo-moral, fate-worse-than-death tale of bondage and ritual mutilation, in which tattoos were acquired to ward off or appease the sexual desires of savages. These tales originated with Olive Oatman, who had been taken captive by Mohave Indians in 1851. Reclaimed at Fort Yuma five years later, she sported traditional chin tattoos which, on her inevitable book and lecture tours, became the feature attraction.

In fact, female settlers in the "New World" may have acquired tattoos in order to make themselves *more* attractive to the native males, who, by and large, showed little carnal interest in these long-skirted, tight-lipped strangers with poor complexions. Young white hunters and woodsmen got the message, however, and took to wearing moccasins and breechcloths.

Spiritual leaders from seventeenth-century Boston couldn't help noticing that, the farther they ventured from urban centers, the more the settlers resembled the natives. Moreover, of the white people captured by natives during the Indian Wars, the number who chose to remain as "savages" when ransomed or recaptured was alarmingly high.

The battle against paganism and heresy in the "New World" seemed to be a losing one. Puritans responded in Jehovah-like fashion — with a ferocious backlash.

Perhaps because paganism represented an active cultural and spiritual threat in North America, and not merely an exotic curiosity, the cult of the noble savage never took hold among the American middle classes, even while it was the height of European fashion. Despite a brief vogue in New York City, in the American heartland tattooing remained the deviant practice of heathens.

Is that what lay behind the campaigns of genocide against the natives, the burning of totem poles and the reservation system? Was it simply the Inquisition American style, the age-old quest to eliminate pagan competition and put an end to the tattooed man?

♥

BOWERY BOYS

By the early twentieth century, tattooing in the "New World" had become a distinctly low-class affectation — the stuff of boxers, stevedores, ex-cons, and other riff-raff.

Designs evolved accordingly. Like comic strips, radio serials and other cultural trash, American tattoo imagery acquired an imaginatively restrictive and conventional style, with a strong line and a lucid symbolic vocabulary. It takes no aesthete to know the meaning of a rose-and-thorn, a skull-and-crossbones, or a nude young woman reclining in a martini glass.

Bowery tattooists, located off Chatham Square at the mouth of the "Thieves' Highway," made a living puncturing crude badges into working-class skin. At first they rented space in barbershops and pool halls; then, as business improved, tattoo parlors appeared with exterior signs declaring, "Black Eyes Made Natural." (It is not clear whether the advertisement applied to insomniacs, chorus girls, or pugilists.)

Master tattooist Samuel F. O'Reilly secured the first U.S. patent on an electric tattoo machine. More sophisticated than Tom Riley's invention a decade earlier, O'Reilly's electric needle combined the technology of a Thomas Edison engraving device with the principle of an electric bell-clapper, and was capable of fifteen hundred punches per minute. (The hand-operated technology, based on the *irezumi* method, could produce a hundred and fifty.)

With his new machine and an expanded range of coloring materials (brick dust, for instance), O'Reilly opened a shop featuring electric tattoos, called "tattaugraphs" to elevate the image, and awarded himself and his assistants the title of "professor."

He enjoyed great success, but made the mistake of defending his patent in court against all comers. As a result, his fortune was exhausted in lawyer's fees. Miserable and broke, O'Reilly died in a fall from a ladder while painting his house in Brooklyn.

CUT ALONG THE DOTTED LINE

Another famous Bowery tattooist, Lew the Jew Alberts, was an ex–wallpaper designer who went into the skin trade part-time during naval service in the Philippines. Upon discharge, Lew took his military clientele into civilian life, creating a demand for his designs. (Lew scrupulously warned his Jewish customers of the Mosaic law against

tattooing, and is said to have sacrificed a good deal of business for his principles.)

His wallpaper background may have lent Lew's designs a certain *flatness*, but it also inspired him to create and market the first mass-produced tattoo designs — the first "flash." These ready-made stencils, printed in editions like, well, wallpaper, were bought and traced by "jaggers" — workaday tattooists with the aesthetics of a plumber — who gave the process its familiar form in the industrialized world. After washing and shaving, the design outline is applied to the skin with an oiled paper (later, an acetate stencil). The outline is then traced, using a machine shaped like a pistol: its butt is two electric coils, its barrel an ink reservoir ending in a needle bar. Groups of fine steel needles vibrate up and down, penetrating the skin to a depth of one thirty-second of an inch, seldom enough to draw significant amounts of blood.

The needle bar usually contains one to four needles for the outline and up to seven for coloring and shading. (A one-needle technique is currently fashionable, but not without controversy. Experienced tattooists claim such a delicate outline will blur over time: a clear, durable outline requires at least three needles.)

The ink is not injected but runs all over the wound, penetrating the skin only where punctured and obscuring the line being traced. This is where guesswork and experience come in. If sufficient depth is not obtained the first time, the line must be retraced; but each repetition further traumatizes the skin, and the resulting scar tissue will cause blurring. Hence, the best tattooists work with surprising speed.

Although the finished tattoo is dressed with an antiseptic salve (usually carbolated Vaseline), some inflammation is apt to occur within a week. A scale then forms, falling away in a few days to reveal the finished design.

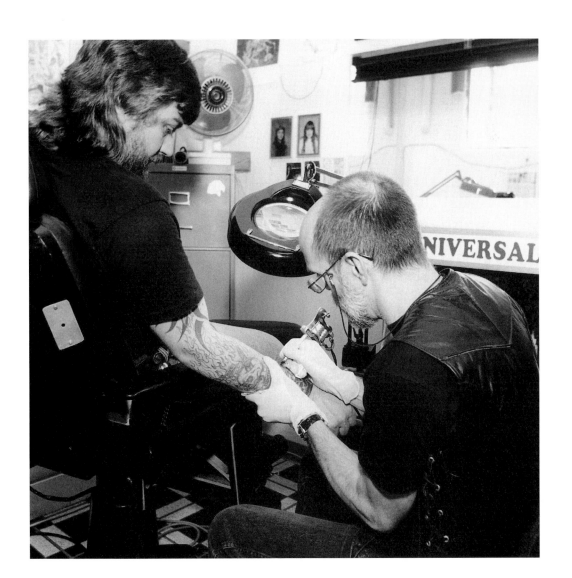

How much does it hurt? Somewhere between an itch and a burn, the degree of pain varies according to the section of skin involved. Thinly covered bone is more painful than, say, the forearm. Psychological variances abound: tattooists share tales of needle-shy football linebackers "doing the chicken" — seizures and fainting far out of proportion to the wound. Women are more apt to take the pain in stride, to make less of a fuss.

Adventures In The Skin Trade

In the absence of a varied civilian clientele, the tattoo parlor concentrated on the creation and execution of military imagery. Each new war produced its distinctive emblems, from the rebel flag to the mushroom cloud. During the Spanish–American War, naval tattoos commemorated the replacement of the three-masted schooner by the steam battleship. Throughout World War I, the most popular tattoo was "Rose of No Man's Land," a comely Red Cross nurse, together with a garland, flag, or religious symbol.

Tattoo iconography during World War II reflected the division of fighting forces into specialized technological units, from submarines to tanks to bombers. (John F. Kennedy had a naval tattoo, which Jackie disliked. It was removed shortly before his assassination.) Tattoos from Vietnam featured the nightmarish, anything-goes psychedelia that characterized that war experience, often combining death imagery with beautiful women, hypodermic needles, and portraits of doomed pop icons such as Jimi Hendrix and Jim Morrison.

The major civilian development throughout the twenties, thirties, and forties followed the rise of the adult newspaper comic strip, which created a new source of wall flash for the Bowery jagger as working-class gentlemen demanded likenesses of Felix the Cat, the Katzenjammer Kids, Mutt and Jeff, and the tattooed sailor then known as "Pop-Eye." Like other lighthearted images, these figures often accompanied popular phrases such as "Oh You Kid" and "So's Your Old Man."

Notwithstanding the title of "professor" and the "permanent" nature of the work, the predictable, hackneyed nature of the average piece of wall flash suggests a market-driven aesthetic rather than the vision of an artist. Even so, design forms can be of greater or lesser "artistic" quality.

Our tendency to dismiss Lew the Jew's wall flash as a degrading development is probably misplaced, for these stencils were less an expression of the tattooist's lack of imagination than an accommodation of the neo-tribal conformism of the client: the average male tattoo recipient wishes to "stand out," but only within narrowly defined margins.

(Like hair stylists and haberdashers, tattooists report that females are invariably more adventurous, spend more time considering their choice, participate more actively in its design and placement, and enjoy more "artistic" results. Men tend to be of the "just do what you think best" school.

This will ring true for anyone who has ever worked in a clothing store: the standard sales pitch to the female shopper stresses the garment's one-of-a-kind nature; the male client responds best to "we sell a lot of those." Unwilling or afraid to discuss the "effeminate" aesthetics of color and line, many men bring their wives for that purpose — whether the purchase is a tie or a tattoo.)

♥

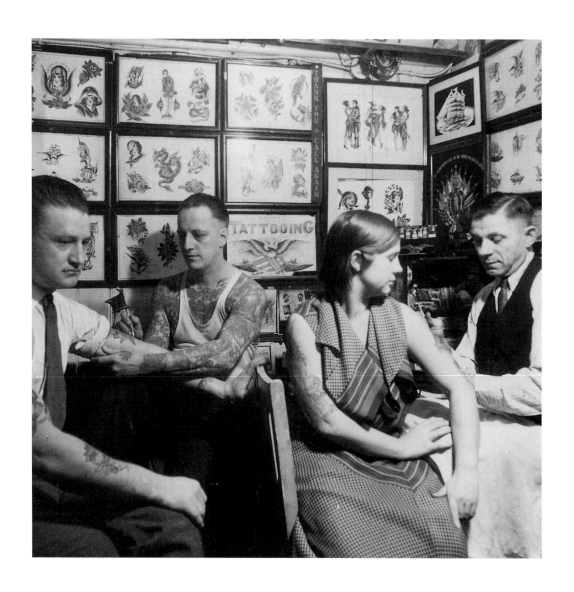

However, if the electric tattoo needle and the mass-produced flash sheet did not vitiate the "artistic" quality of tattooing (in some respects they improved it), together they made the technology and technique marketable as never before. Mail-order ads in *Popular Mechanics* and *Police Gazette*, accompanied by pitches in the tradition of "Grow mushrooms in your basement and earn big bucks!", marketed machines and stencils to anyone with a checkbook and a postage stamp.

Throughout the 1940s and 1950s the most prominent mail-order entrepreneur was an Illinois photographer named Milton Zeis, who marketed "tattoo courses" consisting of an electric machine, needles, inks and accessories, a set of standard tattoo patterns, and an instruction booklet.

Traditionally, tattooists jealously guarded the secrets of their craft — chemical, technical, and aesthetic. One required a connection with an established tattooist just to acquire the equipment, let alone to learn how to use it. Even when an apprenticeship was served in a shop, the beginner mixed pigments, washed up, and practiced on non-human surfaces (grapefruit was a favorite) long before being allowed to do basic fill-in work. Only months later would he be allowed to apply a full tattoo.

The mail-order house bred a new generation of fly-by-night scratchers working, not in shops, but in basements and rooming-house kitchens. A shop acquires a name, a sign, and a reputation. A shop is a physical place to which dissatisfied customers can return with their grievances, whose vulnerability to health regulations and other municipal harassments acts as a regulating constraint. The bootlegger or amateur, with his kit in a suitcase and his office in the nearest tavern, can simply cut and run.

Thanks to mail-order courses and equipment houses such as Spaulding-Rogers

of Voorheesville, New York, tattooing hit the skids: a heart-and-dart was all a 1950s newspaper cartoon needed to signify the ignoble status of the subject.

In 1962, during a "yellow jaundice" epidemic, New York City banned tattoo parlors, virtually equating the craft with the disease. (Tattooing was long suspected of spreading hepatitis, gangrene, and "blood poisoning"; and the unsanitary practice of diluting pigments with the tattooist's saliva is supposed to have transmitted syphilis in Japan and in North America. As either a precaution or a placebo, coloring mixtures often included garlic, believed to ward off germs.)

With the New York ban in effect, the industry was assumed to be dead and buried, deservedly gone the way of the bone in the nose as a relic of a more barbarous time.

Who would have predicted that, three decades later, primitive adornments — tattooing, scarification, branding, and body piercing — would surge back into vogue, under the aegis of a so-called "New Age"?

It is — last stage of all —
When we are frozen up within, and quite
The phantom of ourselves
To hear the world applaud the hollow ghost
Which blamed the living man.

— MATTHEW ARNOLD, 'GROWING OLD'

THE TATTOOED BOY: FOUR   ♥

WHEN THE TATTOOED BOY VANISHED FOREVER, HE LEFT YOU WITHOUT AN ALTERNATIVE role model. Chameleon that you were, you scurried for cover and faded from view.

You looked more carefully at the world around you — how people who fit in walk, talk, and dress. You cultivated the hairstyle sported by a popular television star. You wore shirts with the correct roll of the collar, beneath the correct sweater — sleeves pushed up, not rolled, above the correct amount of forearm. Your hems were the correct length above precisely scuffed loafers. Your finger displayed the correct signet ring. Your mouth produced the correct casual greeting, the correct smile, the correct banter. You put on or took off the correct amount of weight.

Although you continued to learn nothing, your grades improved magically, thanks to study aids designed to teach the appearance of learning. Among administrators and teachers, you stood as living proof that the educational system was effective and meaningful.

With triumphantly average grades you entered university, where you disappeared in an overcrowded faculty. You graduated in the middle of your class. Your mother cried with relief.

After employment interviews in which you stressed your compatibility with all prevailing winds, you accepted a position. At social gatherings, you constructed casual, nonthreatening conversations on neutral topics, leaving a vaguely positive impression of someone harmless. You visited your dentist regularly.

Your work was neither skillful enough to cause resentment among your peers nor so mediocre as to arouse the attention of your superiors. You cultivated the reputation of someone the company could count on — a diligent member of that faceless army, scouting for allies and opponents, treading softly, leaving no tracks.

The economy was robust then. One had but to show up in the morning and smile, and security would ensue.

Those were the days.

But in an economic downturn, the need for invisibility and caution presses more urgently. Riding out a trough in the business cycle, your superiors scanned the office for someone other than themselves to blame. You were in the open that day. Like a jacked deer staring blindly at the headlights of an oncoming vehicle, you were spotted, then flattened. Shrinking profits, declining productivity, low morale — everything became your fault.

You weren't bad or lazy. Worse: you were a failure, a free-market leper. It would be better if you had never been born.

From your workstation you were led past the averted gaze of your colleagues (hunkered in deep cover), to the sparsely furnished, temporary office of an out-placement consultant, a recent graduate on a short-term contract.

You sat, in a state of shock, in the front seat of your Toyota, in your soon-to-be-vacated parking spot, clutching your severance package and a glowing recommendation in your sweaty fist. Ruin comes in many flavors today. In parking lots the world over, bewildered people stare at their rearview mirrors, wondering what happened.

That was the moment you realized that you were alone in this life and had always been alone. You had disappeared but had not merged; your individuality, such as it was, remained stubbornly intact.

You stared at your reflection, shocked to discover that, beyond a slight bewilderment around the eyes, your face was the same face that had consumed its poached egg that morning. It was the same face that had stared into the mirror over the bathroom sink years and years ago, brushing its teeth, wondering what it would look like when it grew up. Your hands on the steering wheel, despite kitchen scars and the odd liver spot, were the same hands that had gripped the handles of your trike as you peddled around the playground.

The skin is the largest organ of the human body. Where was the visible counterpart, the external evidence, of your particular life?

Suddenly you understood why Van Gogh cut off his ear in the shaving mirror. You'd do the same thing if you had a straight razor, not a Philishave.

And that was when your mind went back to the tattooed boy.

HE WAS DRINKING AT THE TIME

Born in 1763, the son of a lawyer, Jean Bernadotte joined the revolutionary French army at age seventeen. He was active in many campaigns throughout the 1790s, then served under Napoleon between 1805 and 1809, with such distinction that he rose to the rank of general, then became marshal of France. Talk about upward mobility.

In 1810, paralyzed by a power vacuum, the Swedes consulted Napoleon, who happened to be the most powerful leader in Europe. Seeking a foreign policy favorable to France, Napoleon recommended his pal Jean, who was promptly elected crown prince. In 1818, unable to speak a word of Swedish, Bernadotte was crowned King Charles XIV of Sweden and Norway.

Some twenty-five years later, old King Charles lay in bed, surrounded by courtiers and in deteriorating health. When the royal physician recommended a restorative bleeding, the ailing king, to the astonishment of his entourage, became visibly flustered and demanded that everyone but the doctor leave the room.

Alone by the bedside, the puzzled surgeon prepared the needle and rolled up the embarrassed monarch's sleeve, uncovering a French revolutionary tattoo — a Jacobean cap, a skull-and-crossbones, a swastika, and the legend: *Death to Kings.*

THE TATTOOED MAN REDUX

SAILOR JERRY COLLINS OF HONOLULU WAS, WITHOUT DOUBT, THE MOST IMPORTANT TATTOOIST of the twentieth century, the man who took the craft by the scruff of the neck, pulled it out of the gutter, and turned it into art — an expression of the conflicting impulses of East and West, of art and commerce, of Buddha, General MacArthur, and Mickey Mouse.

Born in 1911, he rode boxcars to the west coast of America as a teenager, became an amateur tattooist, then joined the merchant marine on passages to Japan, the Philippines, and Southeast Asia.

In Japan he studied the work of the traditional *irezumi* artist Horioshi, one of a few remaining practitioners of that debased craft, who created high-concept tattoo "suits" from mid-thigh to collar-line — classical images of flowers, spirals, and mythical beasts carefully placed to move with the musculature, then shaded so delicately that they appeared to glow luminously from within. If Horioshi's work was egg tempera on gesso, traditional flash was an acrylic matador on black velvet. Returning to America, Collins settled in Hawaii just in time to witness the bombing of Pearl Harbor. Artistically, the two conflicting visions of Japan fueled his career for the rest of his life.

Entrepreneurially, he was impressed by the marketing strategy of a tattooist named Pinky (Bing Kuan) Yun, who ran a successful shop over the Neptune Bar in Hong Kong. No one-room, one-man storefront operation, Pinky's was a tattoo assembly line; master and assistants disseminated a vast array of designs with the speed and efficiency of a fast-food franchise — or an Italian Renaissance master and his students executing frescoes.

In Sailor Jerry's Honolulu shop, George Burchett met Pinky Yun, in an upscale, commercial operation somewhere between a hair stylist and a dentist, appealing to the better class of client. Collins executed fresh adaptations of conventional flash and developed his own range of inks from the superior pigments found in other American print media. He also created techniques for executing these images extremely quickly, causing minimal pain and trauma to the skin while achieving maximum definition. Competing work appeared crude, simplistic, and hazy.

By offering discount rates for large-scale body work (and sometimes working for free), Collins attracted more adventurous (or eccentric) clients, and gradually distanced his work from conventional wall flash. Adapting Japanese techniques to the electric needle and other technical innovations, he became the first American *irezumi* artist.

♥

A mysterious, irascible, independent fellow of some charisma, outside the shop Collins played lead saxophone with a Honolulu swing band, and hosted an all-night talk show under the name "Old Ironsides."

Sailor Jerry's prime motive, artistic considerations aside, was the all-American urge to bounce the competition. He was notoriously cranky and jealous of his trade secrets; in later years he took fiendish delight in using his celebrity to throw the industry into confusion, spreading erroneous information out of spite.

Nursing a lifetime resentment over Pearl Harbor, he sought vengeance against the Japanese by beating Horioshi at his own game. He would use Eastern aesthetic techniques to express American themes, accumulating a surrealistic dream culture of current Americana to ultimately replace Japanese dream imagery reproduced faithfully since the Edo period. Sailor Jerry transformed *irezumi* into an art form as American as the animated cartoon and jazz.

By this time, critics and the American cultural cognoscenti, led by the French left wing, scorned traditional distinctions between "art" and "entertainment" as a product of the class system and of imperial hegemony. Popular entertainments such as B-movies, comic books, and jazz were no longer cheap and dirty populist exploitation; they were "art." Just as Jerry Lewis, Walt Disney, and Louis Armstrong gained artistic respect, by the 1960s Sailor Jerry became recognized as an Artist. Clients flew to Honolulu to acquire "a Sailor Jerry" the way they bought "a Warhol."

A new breed of tattooist drifted into the profession: disaffected art-school types, beaten down by the calcified art establishment, eager to appropriate commercial pop imagery — on record covers, posters, and human skin — and call it art.

During the brief psychedelic era, tattooed flowers, butterflies, and other symbols of peace and love enjoyed a vogue among the flower children of San Francisco, until reality dawned: unlike acid, rock, and revolution, you can turn a tattoo on, but you can't turn it off.

The new generation of tattooists — Lyle Tuttle (who carved a heart and a floral bracelet on Janis Joplin), Don Ed Hardy, and he of the very sixties pseudonym "Cliff Raven" — reverently hung about Sailor Jerry's studio, picking up hints from the truculent master. Then they returned to the mainland as Serious Artists — like comics illustrators, poster designers, and other commercial artists — to become "significant" to a stoned counterculture capable of finding meaning in a tin of Campbell's soup.

With the end of the Vietnam War, flower children sprouted serious philosophical foliage as environmentalists (Greenpeace) and seekers (Transcendental Meditation, Gestalt), as the Beatles generation made the transition from "All You Need Is Love" to "Get Back to Where You Once Belonged."

As an all-purpose image bank, tattooing mutated accordingly: its antediluvian, primitive aspect gave rise to a style of tattooing that would have deeply puzzled Sailor Jerry, designed to appeal to the seeker, the romantic who finds timeless wisdom in anything over a hundred years old.

Just as ex-hippies claimed Buddhist roots to their nascent pacifism and native Indian roots to their back-to-the-land ethic, no tattooist worthy of the needle failed to make his spiritual quest to Japan, Oceania, or New Guinea, to absorb the ancient mysteries and to be "authentically" tattooed at the hands of the "masters."

This primal, purist version of the craft found a mass-market audience by the 1980s, when rock and roll bands such as The Stray Cats, Guns n' Roses, and The Red Hot Chilli Peppers acquired tattoos as a feature of their neo-savage persona.

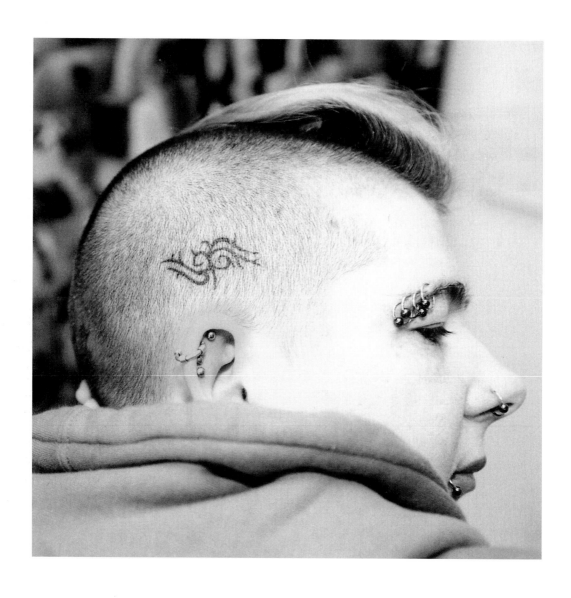

As the music industry became more corporate and profit-driven, and contract employees of Sony and Time-Warner churned out "product" according to predetermined radio playlists, it became a challenge for the front-line troops to convince record buyers of their pure intentions. Tattoos demonstrated a social commitment belied by their business dealings, as though beneath the sycophantic banality of the "product" beat the heart of Cain.

Likewise, their fans, looking forward in life to standardized occupations in the electronics and service industries (if they got a job at all) peppered their bodies with savage and satanic imagery, in the hope that the devil in them would endure.

In a phenomenon not unlike the "tattoo rage" a century ago, tattooing moved upmarket in the 1990s — the *faux*-proletarian decade of The Gap, in which heads of state wear denim shirts. Tattoo parlors sprouted in the better sections of major cities — by-appointment-only operations in university neighborhoods, next to used-clothing boutiques, record shops, and acupuncture clinics — not unlike the Mayfair "tinting" parlors of George Burchett and Sutherland MacDonald.

Such establishments cater to a Generation X clientele seeking to appropriate the native plumage of the urban jungle and display it as their own. For a generation in search of a distinctive logo, a tattoo complements nipple, navel, and tongue piercing as an effective way to get a rise out of Mom and Dad.

Whether "back to the land" or "out of my face," tattoo parlors have become fashionably correct, taking on the pretentiousness of an art gallery, the mustiness of a museum, and the superficial cachet of *haute couture*. At charity benefits, shoulder tattoos peep coyly from under sequined straps; in *Vanity Fair* ads, tattooed hands stroke perfumed bodies in overpriced jeans; and no male show-business personality with half a bicep would roll up his sleeve in public without at least an eagle to display.

If the experience of receiving a tattoo retains any of its rite-of-passage significance, it is the transition from outsider to insider, from un-cool to cool. Suddenly, *everyone* is doing it, darling.

But not for long. The fact of its lifelong permanence sets a tattoo apart from other fashion acquisitions. Sooner or later, as predictably as the next phase of the moon, the tattoo vogue will wane and something else will take its place as the badge of the cognoscenti. Rings will disappear from ears, noses, nipples, and navels, and punctures will fill with scar tissue. But tattoos will remain, like a dirty secret.

In the late 1920s, when the "tattoo rage" finally abated, Lady Randolph Churchill took to covering her snake tattoo with a bracelet. Indeed, the comparative modesty of women's fashions in the 1930s and 1940s may have arisen partly from the desire to cover tattoos, once so daring and doughty, now grown dowdy and *déclassé*.

The road to excess leads to the palace of wisdom . . . for we never know what is enough until we know what is more than enough.

— WILLIAM BLAKE

WHAT NEXT?

Imagine a photograph of a white male's naked torso. The intrepid fellow had the head and shaft of his penis surgically split, so it forms a "Y." He then pierced and attached a ring to each half of the corona, which he clipped to two chains of surgical steel. These

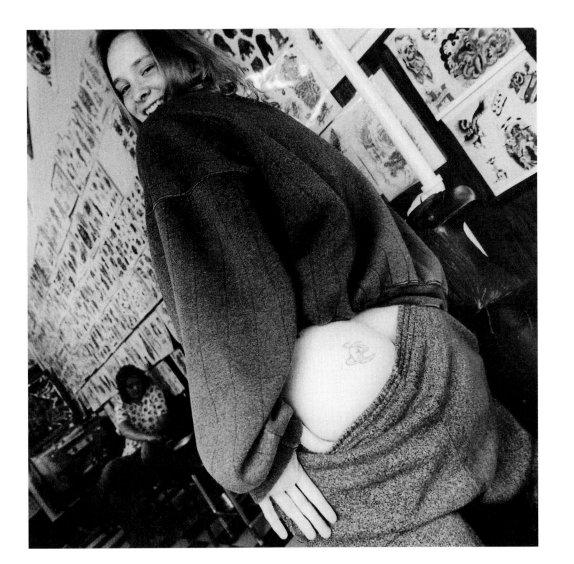

he fastened to rings in his nipples. In the accompanying text, Carl Carroll boasts that customizing his erection has enabled his sexual partners to enjoy "better female orgasmic feelings." He promotes his self-mutilation as archivally significant, a revival of an ancient Australian aboriginal rite.

Jehovah, where are you when we need you?

The God of Genesis made it possible for a human being, naked in an empty room, to sin. Our bodies belonged to Him. They were on loan, to be maintained in good condition. You don't customize a borrowed car.

Without Him, we have no moral yardstick for the "victimless sin," no accepted standard for euthanasia, suicide, abortion, drugs, pornography, sexual preferences, and body alteration. We may find some or all of these practices repugnant, but they do not involve the destruction or theft of somebody else's property.

All we have to go by is that shuddering wince that says a given action is "wrong."

In the late twentieth century we bought out the lease on our bodies; they became our own. With the disintegration of the social order, we scramble toward both past and future, splintering into political, social, and sexual tribes, with our distinctive myths, rituals, and markings. And as society subdivides, the ante goes up. For punks of the late 1970s, pink hair and a safety pin through the nostril were enough to set them apart; now it's tongue piercing.

Brace yourself.

Oh, well. Social disintegration may not be as comfy as stability, but at least it's more interesting. Perhaps there will come a time when we are no longer afraid of our potential diversity, when we have tasted ourselves in all flavors, when everyone has a different tattoo.

JUST WHAT HE ALWAYS WANTED

Lyle Tuttle, who now operates a "tattoo museum" in San Francisco,
made a pilgrimage to Samoa to undergo a five-day marathon of pe'a body tattooing —
detailed basket-like designs from knee to navel. The ordeal claimed the life of
one of his companions, in a hideous scene involving intestines protruding from the
belly button — the young man died of internal injuries and infection. Sighed Tuttle,
"He moaned, tried to speak, then *died* for what he wanted most, a *pe'a*!"

THE TATTOOED BOY: FIVE

♥

YOU SLINK FURTIVELY THROUGH A DECOMPOSING COMMERCIAL NEIGHBORHOOD. YOU ARE unnerved — not because of the crime rate, but because this is where you always feared you would end up, on the shoulder of life's highway, wheels in the ditch, with no place to go.

These grimy storefronts of pawn shops, taverns, and the temporary offices that cash welfare and tax-refund checks are the territory of the bottom-feeder, the trickle-down scavenger who picks through the garbage.

A haberdasher's window covered with yellow film displays ghostly torsos in outdated sports coats, shirts, and ties made by manufacturers who long ago surrendered to Korea. A corner grocery displays peeling ads for cigarettes and discontinued breakfast cereals, having become a covert pharmacy with its shelves stocked with budget euphoria — Lysol, bay rum, and Sterno.

In the rare green spaces sit tired men with Safeway carts full of dumpster treasures. Former construction workers and warehouse clerks lounge in secondhand polyester sportswear from the thrift shop, looking like dissipated golfers after a long, difficult round.

You quicken your pace. You must believe that these people are here for reasons other than pure chance. Otherwise, it could happen to you.

"Dragon Tattoo," says the sandwich board, "Custom Tattooing," and, without irony, "A Touch of Class." A plate-glass window displays the wall flash — skulls, flowers, and pennants, buxom women, predatory animals, and skeletal bikers. A small sign says, "Custom Work." On the door is a warning: "No Food, Animals, or Children under 18."

You open the door tentatively, as though not to wake the occupant. A bell jangles inside, incongruously, as in a country barbershop.

Sheets of flash in protective plastic paper the walls, in a room dominated by a red Kawasaki motorcycle. A broken pinball machine crouches in the back corner, unplugged, beside an exhausted sofa. A medicinal aroma creeps through the cigarette haze, creating a mysterious herbal atmosphere.

The shop consists of a small waiting area and an inner room, separated by an open counter. From behind the counter you hear the intermittent, dental buzz of an electric needle. You cross the linoleum floor and peer inside, carefully, like a voyeur at a windowsill.

A woman stretches languidly atop a blood-and-ink-flecked bath towel, on a cushioned table not unlike an ironing board. Her blouse is open, revealing her black brassiere.

The tattooist, bent over her white stomach, etches a jagged black silhouette just beneath her ribcage. Above the surgical gloves, his bare arms are heavily tattooed — an indistinguishable pattern of blue, orange, and red that make his forearms appear scaled, like the muscular legs of a lizard.

You are embarrassed, as though you have blundered into the wrong bedroom in a foreign hotel. The woman watches you dreamily, half-focusing on your forehead with an expression somewhere between pleasure and pain.

The tattooist speaks without looking up: "What can I do for you?"

He is younger than you expected, with the modified shag haircut favored by working-class men with Kawasaki motorcycles. His tattoos stop abruptly at wrist and neckline: when he puts on a jacket, he could pass for a construction worker on his way out for a beer.

"Well?"

In this alien environment you can only babble: "I'm interested in . . . I'm thinking about . . . I . . . ."

He sets the electric needle down carefully, turns, and looks you over with a practiced eye. Whatever your story, he has heard it before. He goes to the back of the shop and produces a number of hardbound books, which he tosses onto the counter.

"Look through these. Look at the wall flash. Prices are at the bottom corner. Take your time."

He returns to the table and wipes her stomach with a cloth. The electric needle whines as he resumes his curiously sensuous work.

Much has been made of the sexual nature of a procedure involving an active and a passive partner, the marriage of pleasure and pain, and the penetration of a liquid. As a sexual initiation rite in "primitive" cultures, the experience is thought to put a social stamp on the most intimate act by approximating the sensations involved.

The expression on the face of the woman does nothing to contradict this theory.

Some of the designs on the wall go back to Lew the Jew and even Sutherland MacDonald. Other images derive from heavy-metal album covers — pseudo-satanist collages of rampaging death figures. Several are blatantly misogynist: well-endowed female death figures, symbolic representations of a vagina as a toothy trap, a weapon, or a savage beast. Nearby are likenesses of Presley, Dean, Monroe, and more recent designs, abstract silhouettes of Tahitian, Celtic, and Asian origin, in a single color. The prices range from thirty dollars for a simple cartoon character to three hundred dollars for a six-inch Japanese-style dragon.

The illustrated volumes you spread out on the coffee table are not of specific tattoos, but of patterns and motifs — geometric Egyptian suns and animals (with their art deco derivatives), Arabic birds and flowers, Asian reptiles and fish, and Celtic crosses, dogs, and dragons — derived from knot work, engravings, petroglyphs, building façades, fabrics, and other ancient or current crafts.

Other customers join you in the waiting room. You find each one, in some way, alarming. Like patients at a clinic you glance at one another, trying to guess the disease.

Having completed the woman's stomach, the tattooist covers the wound with an antiseptic gel, then with what looks like a piece of Saran Wrap, held in place with tape. She pays in cash, looking relaxed and pleased.

He pockets the bills, changes needles, rubs talcum powder on his hands, and puts on a new pair of surgical gloves.

"Who's next?"

GARFIELD THE CAT

A perspiring, flabby girl of about nineteen, who would be pretty after a spell at a weight-loss clinic, clutches the hand of her boyfriend, a young man with a spidery mustache and jagged workman's fingernails.

Stamped on the girl's forehead in ink, like a grade of beef, is the image of Garfield, the cartoon cat. The tattooist sizes her up, evenly.

"I don't do foreheads."

"I don't want it on my forehead. I want it here." She points to her checked blouse, just above her almost matronly right breast.

"You want me to take a stencil off your forehead and tattoo your right tit?"

She giggles. "No. I brought the stamp with me. See?" She holds up a small plastic ink stamp, triumphantly.

The tattooist examines the stamp suspiciously. "So what did you put it on your forehead for?"

She shrugs. "For fun."

♥

The boyfriend grins at the tattooist. "She's crazy." This is a compliment: beneath the melancholic exterior is an audacious nonconformist.

The tattooist nods abruptly. "Thirty-five dollars."

She looks anxiously up at her boyfriend, who pats her arm. She unbuttons her blouse, exposing one shoulder. On her breast, just above the brassiere, is a small flower.

The tattooist rubs alcohol over the area with a piece of gauze, and carefully places the stamp on her shoulder, to keep it from crowding the flower: "That about right?"

She nods. "What do you think, Arlen? Think that's good?"

"That's good."

The tattooist picks up his needle and revs the motor a couple of times. The machine whines as he sets to work.

You want to stand up, wave your arms, and shout, "Stop! Don't do it!" But women far younger and crazier marry, become pregnant, consume cigarettes, and slash their wrists. Why not a tattoo of Garfield the Cat?

Garfield is furry and plump, passive and sly, content to be fed and petted. Garfield is her totem. The tattoo will transfer his qualities magically to her.

Her boyfriend strokes her neck gently with nicotine fingers.

The tattooist is all concentration and precision, his left hand squeezing her upper arm to hold it steady. The flesh bubbles around the rubber thumb. Beneath an inky smear the outline gradually appears. The girl shows no sign of pain; she watches the face of her boyfriend above her with solemn, watery eyes.

Then the whine of the needle stops.

"You want me to do some shading? Give it some depth?"

She looks at the blob of ink and blood. "No, that's good. Isn't it, Arlen?"

Arlen shrugs.

The tattooist pauses, needle in midair. "You sure? Shading is included in the price."

"No. Just the line is good."

He nods, scoops some salve from a jar, and smears it over the fresh tattoo. "You want a bandage? Don't scab up too bad, do you?"

"No. I don't scab up too bad." For some reason, she's proud of this.

The boyfriend produces a twenty and three fives. The tattooist returns a five to the girl: "I'll give you a discount. For the shading."

"Thanks." The boy and girl smile awkwardly.

The encounter is over. The tattooist, changing needles, waves goodbye without looking up.

They leave the shop, holding hands: the fat girl, Arlen, and Garfield the Cat.

♥

ROSE PETALS

A thin, deeply tanned young man with thick glasses and the furtive, slightly alarmed look of a squirrel wishes to have his vacation souvenir repaired: a shoulder badge of an eagle, a baroque sun with human features, and a garland of flowers. The single-needle lines are merging into smudges, and the tattoo is only two months old.

The tattooist explains the problem: too much detail. He makes sympathetic noises, but refuses to repair the tattoo; the shop covers only its own work. He speaks vaguely of artistic integrity and professional ethics.

The client becomes visibly nervous and blurts out his real request: "Do you do the pubic area?"

A long pause. Sensing encouragement, the client becomes enthusiastic. "I'd like rose petals in my pubic hair."

Evenly, the tattooist points out that the shop lacks the facilities for such intimate work. And some areas of skin take a line better than others. And there is the pain.

"Pain's no problem. I have morphine. . . ."

A young Asian man wants his company logo tattooed on his chest. With the patience of a career counselor, the tattooist describes the current economic uncertainty, the inevitable career changes, and the need for flexibility.

In both cases a faint aura of ethical tension permeates the transaction, yet the moral is unclear: the tattooist cheerfully carves a supermarket bar code on a shaved head and leaves a red-eyed rat skulking on the shoulder blade of a pretty teenager. Why are these more acceptable than a company logo or rose petals on the groin?

The clients come and go; not one of them makes a choice you approve of.

You think back to the tattooed boy, his "hot" and "cold," the incompetent nude on his forearm. How does he feel about these tattoos today? Do they transcend judgment, having enabled him to withstand a psychic battering with his identity intact?

A tattoo is not your father's birthmark, your mother's tendency to worry, or your uncle's leaning to excess. You can't blame your tattoo on anybody else. This mark will be here, for life, because you want it now. An indelible moment of conscious choice.

The tattooist removes his blood-and-ink-stained surgical gloves, tosses them into the wastebasket, changes needles, and peers over the counter. At you.

"Next?"

♥

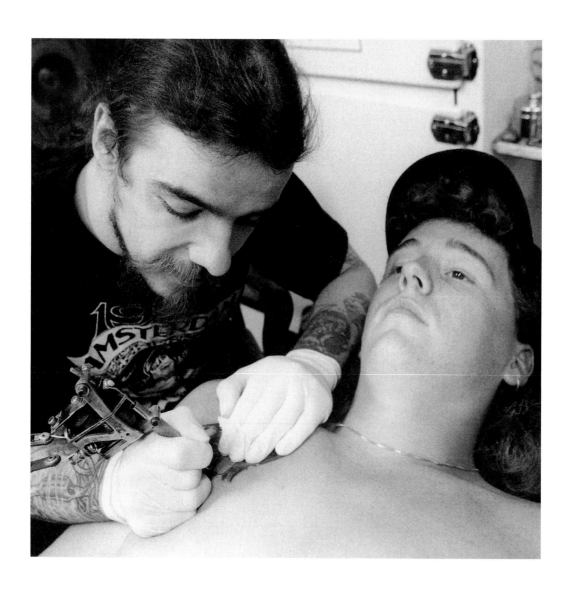

The Tattooist

An instrument, an unseen hand,
Carves a mark for every year;
Another smooth escape is planned,
To see another line appear;
Pose upon the conquered hill,
Take a bow to public praise;
An awkward artist sketches still
The jagged shapes of bygone days;
Squint to see a sweet mirage,
Forge an adolescent strut;
The cosmetician's camouflage,
The plastic surgeon's kinder cut

Will not erase the mark within —
Time's sharp needle, life's soft skin.

— J.G.

CAPTIONS FOR ARCHIVAL ILLUSTRATIONS

PAGE 3 AND COVER: A mythical dragon tattoo on a Japanese woman.

PAGE 8: A Dyak woman of Borneo.

PAGE 14: This blacksmith, photographed in 1942, claimed to be the most tattooed man in the British Army.

PAGE 20: Siberian Eskimos.

PAGE 21: A tattooist and his client in southern Italy.

PAGE 23: A tattooed mummified head.

PAGE 35: A Japanese tattoo artist at work in 1946.

PAGE 37: A British officer being tattooed in Japan.

PAGE 40: George Burchett, "King of Tattooists."

PAGE 43: An American flapper has a heart tattooed on her thigh in 1929.

PAGE 45: The much-tattooed back of David Warford, one of Roosevelt's original Rough Riders.

PAGE 49: Tattooist Charlie Wagner and some of his clients, circa 1942.

PAGE 75: A British woman stands ready to defend her people against the Roman invasion.

PAGE 93: New York tattooist John Conway adds another tattoo to his wife's leg in 1926.

PAGE 104: An old-fashioned American tattoo parlor.

PAGE 106: San Francisco tattoo artist Lyle Tuttle and two of his clients in 1971.

BIBLIOGRAPHY

Burchett, George, and Peter Leighton. *Memoirs of a Tattooist*. London: Pan Books, 1960.

Brain, Robert. *The Decorated Body*. New York: Harper & Row, 1979.

Ebin, Victoria. *The Body Decorated*. London: Thames & Hudson, 1979.

Hardy, D.E., ed. "New Tribalism." In *Tattootime* #1. Honolulu: Hardy-Marks Publications, 1988.

_____. "Tattoo Magic." In *Tattootime* #2. Honolulu: Hardy-Marks Publications, 1988.

_____. "Music & Sea Tattoos." In *Tattootime* #3. Honolulu: Hardy-Marks Publications, 1988.

_____. "Life and Death Tattoos." In *Tattootime* #4. Honolulu: Hardy-Marks Publications, 1988.

Hertz, J.H., ed. *The Pentateuch and Haftorahs*. London: Soncino Press, 1968.

The Holy Bible, Revised Standard Version. Oxford: Oxford University Press, 1989.

Light, Douglas W. *Tattoo Practices of the Cree Indians*. Calgary: Glenbow-Alberta Institute, 1972.

Melville, Herman. *Typee: a Polynesian Life; Omoo: a Narrative*. New York: Viking Press, 1982.

Parry, Albert. *Tattoo*. New York: The Macmillan Company, 1971.

Plath, Sylvia. "The Fifteen Dollar Eagle." In *Johnny Panic and the Bible of Dreams*. New York: Harper & Row, 1978.

Sanders, Clinton. *Customizing the Body*. Philadelphia: Temple University Press, 1989.

Scutt, R., and C. Gotch. *Art, Sex and Symbol*. New York: A.S. Barnes & Co., 1974.

Steward, Samuel M. *Bad Boys and Tough Tattoos*. New York: Haworth Press, 1990.

Thévoz, Michel. *The Painted Body*. New York: Rizzoli International Publications, 1984.

Vale, V., and Andrea Juno, eds. *Modern Primitives*. San Francisco: Research Publications, 1989.

Wroblewski, Chris. *Tattooed Women*. New York: Carol Publishing, n.d.

_____. *Tattoo: Pigments of Imagination*. New York: Alfred Van Der Marck, 1987.

PHOTOGRAPHER'S ACKNOWLEDGMENTS

The photographer wishes to thank all the people who trustingly stood in front of the camera and all the tattoo artists who generously participated in this project. The tattooists are:

Geoff Briggs, Crystal Image Tattooing, Victoria, BC (p. 80, 87)
Cam Von Cook, Sacred Heart Tattoo, Vancouver, BC (p. 5)
Lannie Glover, Fantality, Toronto, ON (p. 7, 9, 83, 111, 127)

Michael Hanson, Skin Dimensions, Winnipeg, MB (p. 132)

Zain Hull, Universal Tattooing, Victoria, BC (p. 64 right)

Vyvyn Lazonga, Dermagraphics, Seattle, WA (p. 53, 58, 71, 73, 89, 90, 99, 117)

Rosalle McNeil, Mum's Tattoo, North Vancouver, BC (p. 120, 144)

Joe Quin, Salt Spring Island, BC (p. 2)

Trevor Quin, Salt Spring Island, BC (p. 125)

Daemon Rowanchilde, Urban Primitive, Toronto, ON (p. 63)

Adam Sky, Sacred Heart Tattoo, Vancouver, BC (p. 11, 108 far right)

Jeff Tulloch, Mum's Tattoo, North Vancouver, BC (p. 108 second from right)

Wingate, Port Townsend Tattoo and Fine Arts, Port Townsend, WA (p. 13, 51, 56,
       67 legs only).

Acknowledgment to other artists whose work appears:
p. 29, Mark Vienneau; p. 65, Michael Dick (left); p. 67, Cliff Raven (torso);
       p. 89, Alex Binnie (upper right arm); p. 96, Romeo Vallancourt (right arm);
       p. 108, Jeff Raiser (far left) and Theo Jak (second from left); p. 137, Johnny
       Faulds (left) and Rob Schiffner (right).

Special thanks to Dan McNeil, Garry Peak, Ziggy Harwood, Jean Laskey
       and Raven.